DISEASES & DISORDERS

Autoimmune Disorders

Melissa Abramovitz

LUCENT BOOKS

A part of Gale, Cengage Learning

GALE
CENGAGE Learning

Detroit • New York • San Francisco • New Haven, Conn • Waterville, Maine • London

LIBRARY OF CONGRESS CATALOGING-IN-PUBLICATION DATA

Abramovitz, Melissa, 1954-
  Autoimmune disorders / by Melissa Abramovitz.
    p. cm. -- (Diseases and disorders)
  Summary: "This series objectively and thoughtfully explores topics of medical importance. Books include sections on a description of the disease or disorder and how it affects the body, as well as diagnosis and treatment of the condition"-- Provided by publisher.
  Includes bibliographical references and index.
  ISBN 978-1-4205-0657-0 (hardback)
  1. Autoimmune diseases--Popular works. I. Title.
  RC600.A28 2011
  616.97'8--dc22
                                                    2011006555

Lucent Books
27500 Drake Rd.
Farmington Hills, MI 48331

ISBN-13: 978-1-4205-0657-0
ISBN-10: 1-4205-0657-9

Printed in the United States of America
1 2 3 4 5 6 7 15 14 13 12 11

Printed by Bang Printing, Brainerd, MN, 1st Ptg., 06/2011

Table of Contents

"The Most Difficult Puzzles Ever Devised"

Charles Best, one of the pioneers in the search for a cure for diabetes, once explained what it is about medical research that intrigued him so. "It's not just the gratification of knowing one is helping people," he confided, "although that probably is a more heroic and selfless motivation. Those feelings may enter in, but truly, what I find best is the feeling of going toe to toe with nature, of trying to solve the most difficult puzzles ever devised. The answers are there somewhere, those keys that will solve the puzzle and make the patient well. But how will those keys be found?"

Since the dawn of civilization, nothing has so puzzled people—and often frightened them, as well—as the onset of illness in a body or mind that had seemed healthy before. A seizure, the inability of a heart to pump, the sudden deterioration of muscle tone in a small child—being unable to reverse such conditions or even to understand why they occur was unspeakably frustrating to healers. Even before there were names for such conditions, even before they were understood at all, each was a reminder of how complex the human body was, and how vulnerable.

While our grappling with understanding diseases has been frustrating at times, it has also provided some of humankind's most heroic accomplishments. Alexander Fleming's accidental discovery in 1928 of a mold that could be turned into penicillin has resulted in the saving of untold millions of lives. The isolation of the enzyme insulin has reversed what was once a death sentence for anyone with diabetes. There have been great strides in combating conditions for which there is not yet a cure, too. Medicines can help AIDS patients live longer, diagnostic tools such as mammography and ultrasounds can help doctors find tumors while they are treatable, and laser surgery techniques have made the most intricate, minute operations routine.

This "toe-to-toe" competition with diseases and disorders is even more remarkable when seen in a historical continuum. An astonishing amount of progress has been made in a very short time. Just two hundred years ago, the existence of germs as a cause of some diseases was unknown. In fact, it was less than 150 years ago that a British surgeon named Joseph Lister had difficulty persuading his fellow doctors that washing their hands before delivering a baby might increase the chances of a healthy delivery (especially if they had just attended to a diseased patient)!

Each book in Lucent's Diseases and Disorders series explores a disease or disorder and the knowledge that has been accumulated (or discarded) by doctors through the years. Each book also examines the tools used for pinpointing a diagnosis, as well as the various means that are used to treat or cure a disease. Finally, new ideas are presented—techniques or medicines that may be on the horizon.

Frustration and disappointment are still part of medicine, for not every disease or condition can be cured or prevented. But the limitations of knowledge are being pushed outward constantly; the "most difficult puzzles ever devised" are finding challengers every day.

A Rapidly Multiplying Problem

Autoimmune disorders, which result from the immune system mistakenly attacking the body's own cells, have affected people throughout history. However, the prevalence of these diseases is multiplying at an unprecedented pace in modern times. Autoimmune disease expert Douglas Kerr says in *The Autoimmune Epidemic* that "in some cases, autoimmune diseases are three times more common now than they were several decades ago. These changes are not due to increased recognition of these disorders or altered diagnostic criteria. Rather, more people are getting autoimmune disorders than ever before."[1]

In 1997, from 14 million to 22 million people in the United States had an autoimmune disease. Today, about 50 million Americans, or 20 percent of the population, suffer from one or more of the approximately one hundred known autoimmune diseases. Over 75 percent of these people are female. Autoimmune disorders are now the number two cause of chronic illness in the United States, and they lead to ongoing suffering and death for millions of individuals each year. Associated health care costs total over $100 billion per year and are rising as more and more people are affected.

The incidence of autoimmune disorders is rising in many other countries as well. The occurrence of one autoimmune disease, multiple sclerosis (MS), in Finland, England, Denmark, Scotland, Sweden, and the Netherlands, for example, has tripled since the 1950s. The number of cases of type 1 diabetes has increased by a factor of five in many places throughout the world. But the number of cases of autoimmune diseases is not multiplying to the same extent in all locations. Instead, the most dramatic increases are occurring in industrialized countries.

What Is to Blame?

Experts have varying opinions about what is causing these dramatic and location-specific increases, but most agree that

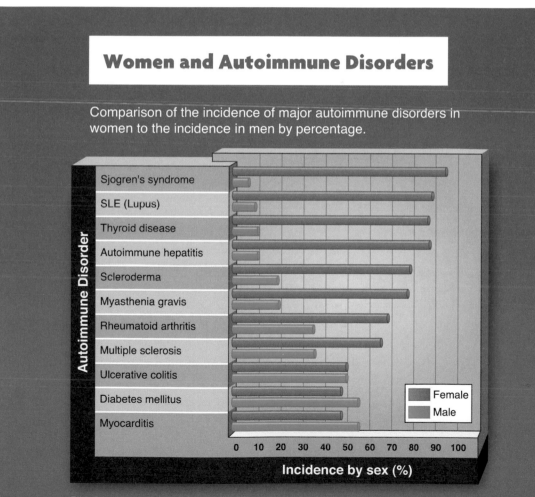

Women and Autoimmune Disorders

Comparison of the incidence of major autoimmune disorders in women to the incidence in men by percentage.

Taken from: Centers For Disease Control and Prevention. www.cdc.gov/NCIDOD/EID/VOLIONO11/04-367-gi.html.
Modified from: C.C. Whitacre. Sex Differences in Autoimmune Disease. Natural Immunology, 2001, pp. 777–780.

it has to do with changes in the environment. As autoimmune disease authority Noel R. Rose of the Johns Hopkins medical institutions states, "The only reasonable explanation is that it is caused by exposure to environmental agents. Unfortunately, we still have relatively little information about the environmental triggers of autoimmunity and about their mechanisms of action."[2]

Some scientists have proposed that chemicals in the air, water, soil, and consumer products, such as pesticides, industrial chemicals, flame retardants in fabrics, plastics, and even nonstick cookware, are responsible. Others believe that heavy metals, viruses, or vaccines play a role. No one, however, has proved which, if any, toxins are actually causing these increases.

Some experts believe that the vast number of toxins to which people are exposed, in addition to individual substances, may be to blame. A 2009 report by the federal Centers for Disease Control and Prevention (CDC) states that ordinary Americans who do not work with toxic chemicals have about 212 potentially harmful chemicals in their blood and urine. While scientists have not proved whether some of these chemicals pose health risks, neurologist Ahmet Hoke of the Johns Hopkins medical institutions points out that their sheer volume may be placing unprecedented demands on the immune system:

> Since the industrial revolution, we've generated hundreds of thousands of new chemicals and released them into our environment. Our ancestors and their immune systems were never exposed to such a complex array of chemical structures. It takes thousands of years to adapt to environmental stresses, but we are now asking our immune system to differentiate between all of these new chemical structures and our own body. A mistake is bound to happen where the immune system recognizes a self epitope [unique chemical identifier] as foreign because it has a close chemical structure to a foreign substance in our environment. This mistake manifests itself as autoimmune disease.[3]

Seeking Evidence

Some evidence that environmental toxins play a role in fueling the rise in autoimmune disorders comes from disease clusters (abnormally high numbers of cases) in places located near sites where industries have dumped large quantities of chemicals or where chemicals have leaked into the air, soil, and water from abandoned businesses. In the 1980s and 1990s, for example, an unusually large number of people in one neighborhood in Buffalo, New York, was diagnosed with or died from the autoimmune diseases lupus, rheumatoid arthritis, scleroderma, type 1 diabetes, and others. Lupus was the most prevalent disease among those affected; seventeen people living on two streets adjacent to a toxic waste site developed it. No one is sure which chemicals were responsible.

Numerous similar clusters and other evidence linking certain toxins to health problems in humans and animals have spurred public health agencies to launch extensive research projects aimed at determining which factors are involved.

Some evidence suggests that environmental toxins have had a role in causing the rise in autoimmune disorders.

The Environmental Protection Agency (EPA), for example, is conducting research to assess precisely how certain toxins and combinations of toxins produce health problems such as autoimmune diseases and cancers. The EPA is also exploring why these problems seem to be more frequent and severe in certain people, such as women and children. Such research has already led to new tools for determining the cumulative effects of chemicals. For instance, researchers affiliated with the EPA's Human Health Research Program developed a scientific method called the Stochastic Human Exposure and Dose Simulation Multimedia Model that enables scientists to predict chemical exposures and their effects without actually exposing people to these chemicals. This information can be used to develop government regulations concerning allowable levels of toxins. Already, new recommendations have been implemented concerning the use of certain pesticides, cleaning products, and fuels.

But autoimmune disease experts and advocates agree that much more research is needed before they understand how and why certain environmental substances may be tied to the growing incidence of these diseases. Until such research yields answers, no one can determine exactly what steps legislators, health care professionals, and the general public must take to control this rapidly multiplying problem.

CHAPTER ONE

What Are Autoimmune Disorders?

Autoimmune disorders occur when the body's immune system attacks the body's own cells or tissues. The word *auto* means "self," and *immune* refers to the body's system of defense against invaders such as bacteria, viruses, cancer, toxins, and other foreign cells or substances. As autoimmune disease expert Douglas Kerr writes, "The soldiers guarding the castle turn and attack it."[4] This autoimmune assault can result in various diseases, depending on which cells are damaged or destroyed.

Some people confuse autoimmunity with allergies, but even though both involve an out-of-control immune response, their targets are very different. An allergy occurs when a person's immune system attacks a foreign substance that is usually ignored by most other people's immune systems. Such substances might be pollen or particular foods, among other things, but they are not the body's own cells.

The Structure of the Immune System

The immune system consists of a network of cells and organs throughout the body that work together to launch and complete an effective defense against invaders. The first line of immune defense consists of cells and chemicals in outer barriers such as the skin, eyes, nose, mouth, and genitals. If a foreign

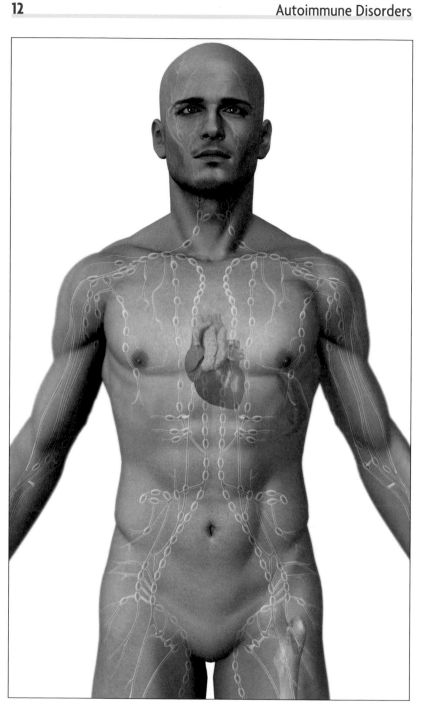

Image of the immune system inside a male torso. Visible are the heart, thymus, the lymphatic system, the spleen, and femur bone.

microorganism or substance gets past these defenses, the internal immune system goes to work.

The immune system has four basic parts: the innate and acquired immune systems, and the cellular and humoral (chemical) immune systems. According to the National Institute of Arthritis and Musculoskeletal and Skin Diseases (NIAMS), "The more primitive innate (or inborn) immune system activates white blood cells to destroy invaders. The innate system alerts the body to danger when it senses the presence of parts that are often found in many viruses and bacteria. The acquired (or adaptive) immune system develops as a person grows. It 'remembers' different invaders so that it can fight them better if they come back."[5]

The humoral immune system consists primarily of antibodies, complement, and cytokines. White blood cells produce antibodies, which are chemicals that attach to and attack specific antigens (foreign proteins or substances). Each antibody attacks one particular antigen.

Over thirty proteins in the so-called complement system assist, or complement, antibodies in their battle. According to *The Encyclopedia of Autoimmune Diseases*, "Complement proteins circulate in the blood in an inactive form. When the first of the complement substances is triggered—usually by an antibody interlocked with an antigen—it sets in motion a ripple effect. As each component is activated in turn, it acts upon the next in a precise sequence of carefully regulated steps known as the *complement cascade*."[6] Complement proteins directly kill microorganisms, attract white blood cells to antigens, help immune cells remember antigens, help trigger antibody formation, produce inflammation, and help the body eliminate dead cells and immune complexes (antibodies attached to antigens).

Cytokines are chemical messengers that work closely with other immune chemicals to stimulate or inhibit immune cells. They also directly interfere with the reproduction of viruses. Common cytokines include interferons and interleukins. Interferons activate immune cells, attack and kill viruses, and interfere with virus reproduction. Different kinds of interleukins can stimulate or inhibit immune cells. Interleukin-2, for example, tells the immune system to produce a type of white blood cell called T cells.

The Cellular Immune System

The cellular immune system is mainly composed of white blood cells, or leukocytes. All leukocytes are produced in the bone marrow (the soft, spongy tissue in the bones' hollow centers) along with other blood cells such as red blood cells, but some leukocytes mature in other organs. Like other body cells, blood cells begin as immature stem cells that can mature into specific cell types after they receive chemical "instructions."

There are two main types of leukocytes: phagocytes and lymphocytes. Each type has several subtypes. Phagocytes engulf, swallow, and poison invading antigens. The subtypes of phagocytes are granulocytes and monocytes. Granulocytes come in three varieties: neutrophils, eosinophils, and basophils. Neutrophils are the most numerous white blood cells. The bone marrow produces trillions each day, but each cell lives for only about a day. Once in the bloodstream, neutrophils are attracted to antigens throughout the body. When they reach an antigen, they surround it and release chemicals to poison it. Eosinophils primarily attack parasites in the skin and lungs. Basophils carry chemicals such as histamine that create inflammation in response to an injury or antigen. Inflammation is the immune system's method of preventing an infection from spreading.

Monocytes secrete chemicals that kill many types of microorganisms. They are especially effective in fighting bacteria and fungi. Monocytes also ingest and remove dead microorganisms and blood cells from the bloodstream and from body tissues, secrete cytokines, and display antigens to other white blood cells. When monocytes migrate from the bloodstream to tissues, they develop into macrophages, which are larger cells that perform these same duties.

Phagocytes, along with a type of lymphocyte called natural killer (NK) cells, are the primary components of the innate im-

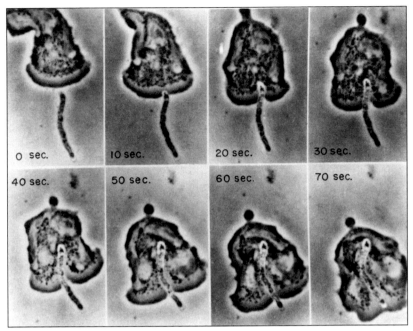

0 sec.	10 sec.	20 sec.	30 sec.
40 sec.	50 sec.	60 sec.	70 sec.

This color-enhanced microscopic view shows a human white blood cell engulfing a bacterium. The whole process takes only seventy seconds.

mune system. Other lymphocytes called B cells and T cells are primarily involved in acquired immunity.

The Lymphatic System

The three subtypes of lymphocytes perform functions that complement and sometimes duplicate what other leukocytes do and, in addition, work closely with organs and tissues collectively known as the lymphatic system. NK cells hunt down and kill antigens by releasing damaging chemicals and also produce cytokines. B cells, so named because most of them mature in the bone marrow, mainly assist in activating the immune response and in producing antibodies. In addition, they can morph into cells called plasma cells, which also produce antibodies, or into memory cells, which remember antigens. T cells, which mature in a small gland behind the breastbone called the thymus, come in three varieties: helper T cells, cytotoxic or killer T cells, and suppressor or regulatory T cells. Helper T cells release cytokines that activate phagocytes and that stimulate B cells to produce antibodies. Killer T cells use deadly chemicals to kill infected body cells so an infection will not spread, and suppressor T cells secrete cytokines that prevent an immune attack from spiraling out of control.

All white blood cells circulate through the bloodstream, but lymphocytes also perform their duties by traveling through a network of nearby vessels called lymphatic vessels. Lymphatic vessels contain a clear fluid called lymph, which transports water, nutrients, and lymphocytes from one lymph node to another. The lymph then drains into the bloodstream through connecting ducts.

Lymph nodes are clusters of lymphocytes that play a big role in the immune defense system. Autoimmune disease expert Robert Lahita writes in *Women and Autoimmune Disease*, "Using a police force as an analogy for the immune system, you might consider the lymph nodes as police precincts that are strategically placed in various parts of the body where the immune system has to be on high alert—for example the tonsils, the ears, the mouth, the genitals, or any area where there might

A diagram of a lymph node. Lymph nodes are strategically placed in the body where the immune system is on high alert, such as the tonsils, ears, mouth, and genitalia.

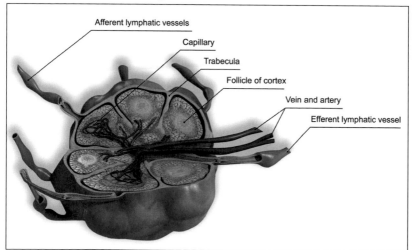

Afferent lymphatic vessels

Capillary

Trabecula

Follicle of cortex

Vein and artery

Efferent lymphatic vessel

be an invasion of a foreign substance or a foreign germ."[7] Immune cells and antigens enter lymph nodes through lymphatic vessels, and once inside, different cells congregate in different areas. This is why lymph nodes often become swollen when the body is fighting an infection.

Other organs and tissues that are part of the lymphatic system include the spleen, which is a fist-shaped organ in the abdomen that contains special compartments where immune cells gather and work, and areas of the appendix, lungs, and digestive organs that also provide a working area for lymphocytes.

The Functions of the Immune System

All these organs, cells, and chemicals interact extensively to perform their intended functions. As the National Institute of Allergy and Infectious Diseases (NIAID) explains,

> Millions and millions of cells, organized into sets and subsets, gather like clouds of bees swarming around a hive and pass information back and forth in response to infection. Once immune cells receive the alarm, they become activated and begin to produce powerful chemicals. These substances allow the cells to regulate their own growth and behavior, enlist other immune cells, and direct the new recruits to trouble spots.[8]

These basic functions can be summarized as recognition, activation and mobilization, regulation, and resolution. In recognition, immune cells analyze identification molecules, called major histocompatability complex (MHC) molecules, that appear on all antigens and cells, to determine which are foreign and which are self. The MHC molecules on human cells are called human leukocyte antigens (HLAs). Each person has a unique combination of HLAs, and an individual's immune cells normally recognize this combination as self and any other identifying molecules as foreign.

B cells, T cells, macrophages, and other cells, called dendritic cells, are all involved in the recognition process. B cells, dendritic cells, and macrophages act as antigen-presenting cells:

Types of Antibodies

Antibodies are chemicals that white blood cells produce to fight specific antigens. Each antibody molecule consists of two parts: the variable part and the constant part. The variable part differs from antibody to antibody. It is designed to attach only to a specific antigen. The constant part is identical among antibodies of the same class. There are five classes of antibodies: IgM, IgG, IgA, IgE, and IgD. Ig stands for immunoglobulin, which is another word for antibody.

Each class of antibody has different functions. White blood cells produce IgM antibodies when they encounter an antigen for the first time, so it is called the primary immune response. When IgM attaches to an antigen, the complement system of chemicals that help destroy the antigen is activated. IgM is present in the bloodstream but not in body tissues. IgG is produced primarily when immune cells encounter an antigen again and "remember" it; thus it is known as the secondary immune response. The secondary response occurs much faster than the primary immune response does. IgG is present in blood and tissues and is also the only type of antibody to cross the placenta from a mother to a fetus.

IgA, IgE, and IgD can be produced at any time in an immune response. IgA exists mainly in body tissues that are lined with a mucous membrane, such as the eyes, nose, mouth, and digestive system. Its primary function is to destroy microorganisms like bacteria and viruses before they escape from these areas. IgE is found in the bloodstream and mostly triggers allergies to certain substances. IgD sits on immature B cells and helps them mature.

They process the identification molecules on the antigens that otherwise would not fit receptors on the T cells' surfaces.

The antigen-presenting cells process these identification molecules by ingesting them and dividing them into pieces. They then combine these pieces with HLA molecules that exist in all body cells. After this, antigen-presenting cells transport and present the combination to nearby T cells. As well as serving to identify body cells as self, HLA molecules also act as the "keys" which fit into T cell receptors. Once the "key" is in place, the T cells determine whether the HLA molecules are alone—in which case they identify the antigen as self—or are combined with other molecules—in which case they identify it as foreign.

In addition to presenting antigens to T cells, B cells also recognize antigens directly. Once B and T cells complete the recognition process, the next phase of the immune attack, activation and mobilization, can begin.

In this phase, some T cells begin killing foreign cells, while others release cytokines that stimulate other leukocytes into action. Some B cells are activated by these cytokines, and others spring into action after they themselves recognize an antigen as foreign. Activated B cells either change into memory cells that remember specific antigens, or into plasma cells that produce antibodies. Antibodies then stimulate phagocytes to ingest antigens and activate complement proteins. Macrophages and neutrophils are also involved in activation—macrophages produce cytokines that attract other leukocytes to the site of an infection, and neutrophils produce fibers that trap antigens to prevent them from spreading throughout the body.

After activation and mobilization succeed in killing off or trapping foreign antigens, the regulation phase begins. Its purpose is to prevent the immune system from damaging its own tissues. The main mechanism by which regulation occurs is through regulatory T cells producing cytokines, such as interleukin-10, that tell other immune cells to back off.

The final step, resolution, primarily involves macrophages. Neutrophils and lymphocytes, other than the B and T cells that become memory cells, begin to die off in response to inhibitory cytokines, and macrophages consume the dead cells and any immune complexes they find. Then the macrophages enter the bloodstream and are eliminated through the digestive system or kidneys.

Different Yet Similar Diseases

Scientists now know that malfunctions in any phase of this immune process can lead to errors that result in autoimmunity. Until the 1950s, though, medical experts believed that autoimmunity was impossible, based on a widely accepted theory known as *horror autotoxicus* (fear of self-poisoning) put forth by immunologist Paul Ehrlich in the early 1900s. But in 1951 Noel R. Rose, then at the State University of New York in Buffalo, made a chance discovery that constituted the first step in disproving Ehrlich's theory and in allowing doctors to identify many diseases as having autoimmune origins. During experiments to purify a thyroid gland protein called thyroglobulin, Rose found that if he injected the protein back into the bodies of rabbits from which it was taken, the animals' thyroid glands became inflamed. He also discovered that the injected thyroglobulin was not directly inflaming the thyroid but was somehow stimulating the animals' immune systems to produce antibodies against their own thyroid tissue. The rabbits developed a disease similar to the human disorder called Hashimoto's thyroiditis, which has since been proved to be an autoimmune disease.

Rose and his colleagues were initially skeptical about these findings. "Ehrlich was my teacher's teacher, and I was reluctant to contravene any of his statements," Rose said in an interview. "However, careful reading of his article pointed out that he was not claiming that autoimmunity did not exist; he rather suggested that there are devices to prevent the damaging effects of autoimmunity."[9]

This reinterpretation, along with further studies that confirmed that autoimmunity was not only possible but that it could affect any organ or tissue in the body, convinced Rose and his associates that their findings were valid. But even then, most doctors did not accept the idea of autoimmunity until the early 1970s, when researchers began realizing that many diseases are autoimmune in nature. Some autoimmune diseases, such as vasculitis, are fairly rare, even with recent increases in prevalence, and affect only thousands of people. Others,

Paul Ehrlich

Paul Ehrlich was born in Strehlen, Germany, in 1854 and obtained his medical degree in 1878. His early research work at the Berlin Medical Clinic focused on staining animal tissues for examination in a laboratory. Some of the techniques he developed are still used today. Later, his work centered on the immune system. His renowned side-chain theory of immunity hypothesized that living cells have receptors called side chains which multiply in response to toxic substances. This theory proved to be wrong but launched a new field of scientific inquiry into the immune system.

In 1899 he began developing "magic bullets," or drugs that specifically attack certain antigens. One drug he developed was the first to be effective against the bacterium that causes syphilis. He also formulated several other theories about immunity; the most famous was his *horror autotoxicus* theory, which stated that the immune system will not attack the body's own cells. In the *Collected Papers of Paul Ehrlich*, he writes, "The organism possesses certain contrivances by means of which the immunity reaction, so easily produced by all kinds of cells, is prevented from acting against the organism's own elements and so giving rise to auto-toxins . . . so that one might be justified in speaking of a 'horror autotoxicus' of the organism." This theory was not disproved until the 1950s.

Ehrlich received many honors and awards for his contributions to medical science and In 1908 was awarded the Nobel Prize for Medicine. He died in 1915 from a stroke.

Quoted in F. Himmelweit. *Collected Papers of Paul Ehrlich*. London: Pergamon, 1956, p. 253.

Dr. Paul Ehrlich won the Nobel Prize for Medicine in 1908 for his work in finding a remedy for syphilis.

like lupus and diabetes, have never been considered to be rare diseases but have increased in prevalence at an alarming rate over the past several decades.

The more than one hundred autoimmune diseases identified to date have varying symptoms and complications, depending on which tissues are involved, but many include common elements such as fatigue, weakness, and pain. Most of these diseases also affect different patients to different degrees; some experience only mild illness, while others become severely disabled. Doctors usually cannot predict how different people will be affected over time.

Some autoimmune diseases, such as type 1 diabetes and antiphospholipid syndrome, are invariably life threatening without treatment, while others like psoriasis can be mild and not lead to critical problems. Whether severe or not, most autoimmune disorders are chronic, or long-term. Symptoms in some may come and go, but the diseases do not go away and in many cases worsen over time. When symptoms suddenly develop or worsen, doctors refer to this as a flare or flare-up. When symptoms disappear, this is known as a remission. If symptoms return after a remission, doctors call it a relapse. Some autoimmune disorders like MS and rheumatoid arthritis involve frequent flares, remissions, or relapses, while others like type 1 diabetes are ongoing chronic diseases that do not let up.

All autoimmune disorders can affect anyone of any age, but many begin during childhood, adolescence, or young adulthood and last a lifetime. Many people who have an autoimmune disease also tend to develop other autoimmune disorders.

Different autoimmune disorders also affect varying numbers of body parts. According to the National Institutes of Health (NIH), "An autoimmune disorder may result in the destruction of one or more types of body tissue, abnormal growth of an organ, or changes in organ function."[10] Doctors classify autoimmune diseases according to whether they affect specific organs or tissue or are widespread throughout the body. Examples of organ-specific diseases are type 1 diabetes, which affects cells in the pancreas; Hashimoto's thyroiditis, which affects cells in the thyroid gland; and Crohn's disease, which attacks cells in the digestive tract. Non-organ-specific diseases include rheumatoid arthritis, which affects joints throughout the body; antiphospholipid syndrome, which involves widespread blood clots; vasculitis, in which blood vessels become inflamed; and lupus, which can involve the skin and diverse organs like the kidneys and heart.

Examples of Common Autoimmune Diseases

Some of the more common autoimmune diseases that illustrate the diversity of affected body parts and symptoms are Sjogren's syndrome, rheumatoid arthritis, multiple sclerosis, lupus, and type 1 diabetes. Sjogren's syndrome, named after the Swedish doctor who identified it, is one of the most prevalent autoimmune disorders, affecting about 4 million Americans, 90 percent of whom are female. Sjogren's involves an attack on moisture-producing glands throughout the body. Typical symptoms are dry eyes, nose, mouth, and skin; widespread pain; and fatigue. Dry eyes can become ulcerated; dry mouth can lead to tooth decay, sores, a cracked tongue, and changes in taste sensations; and a dry nose can bleed and allow bacteria to multiply. Dryness in other organs such as the kidneys, lungs, gastrointestinal system, and nervous system can lead to numbness, nausea, infections, and memory problems.

Rheumatoid arthritis affects about 1.3 million people in the United States and involves an immune attack on the joints, resulting in pain, stiffness, swelling, deformity, thickening of the tissue lining the joints, and bone destruction. The disease can begin at any age but usually starts between ages twenty and fifty. Young children can get a form of rheumatoid arthritis called juvenile arthritis. Some affected people have mild symptoms, but many experience frequent flares and severe pain and disability. Many cannot use their hands and have trouble walking.

In multiple sclerosis, the immune system attacks and destroys the lining of nerve cells in the brain and spinal cord. This lining is called the myelin sheath; thus MS is known as a demyelinating disease. The attack results in patches of inflamed tissue

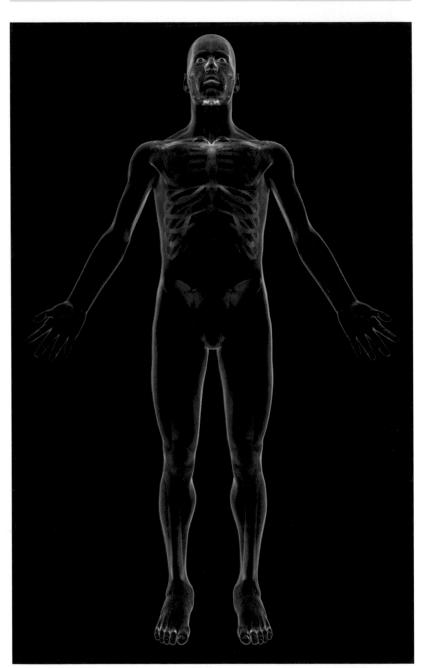

Areas of joint pain caused by rheumatoid arthritis are highlighted in red. It attacks joints, resulting in pain, stiffness, swelling, deformities, thickening of joint tissue, and bone destruction.

called plaques, which interfere with the ability of nerve cells to transmit and receive signals from other nerve cells. Depending on where the plaques are located, patients can experience a variety of symptoms. Plaques in the area of the brain called the cerebrum, for example, may lead to problems with thinking, memory, and sensation. Plaques in the cerebellum, which controls balance and movement, can interfere with these abilities. Plaques in the spinal cord can result in numbness, paralysis, or lack of control of certain organs like the bladder.

Some people with MS experience ongoing deterioration and disability, while others have milder symptoms and slower disease progression. Doctors distinguish four main types of MS that differ in the pattern and severity of flare-ups. About four hundred thousand people in the United States have MS, and the disease is two to three times more common in females than in males.

Lupus affects over 1.5 million Americans, of whom 90 percent are female. The disease affects a wide variety of organs, from the skin to the heart and lungs to the kidneys. When only the skin is affected by rashes or small sores, doctors refer to the disease as discoid lupus. This form of lupus is often mild and not life threatening. The more common form called systemic lupus erythematosus (SLE), on the other hand, can affect any organ and may be life threatening. Symptoms of SLE vary widely and may resemble symptoms of many other diseases. For this reason, medical experts have dubbed SLE "The Great Imposter." Symptoms may include fatigue, headache, swollen joints, fever, anemia (deficiency of red blood cells), chest pain, a butterfly-shaped rash on the face, hair loss, mouth or skin ulcers, mental confusion, and blood-clotting problems. Professional baseball player Tim Raines, who developed SLE in 1999, for example, experienced extreme fatigue and swollen ankles and knees. Tests revealed that the lupus had attacked his kidneys.

Type 1, or insulin-dependent, diabetes usually begins in childhood or adolescence and affects over 3 million Americans. It is one autoimmune disorder that affects males and females pretty much equally. It differs from type 2 diabetes, which has similar symptoms but usually results from obesity rather than autoimmunity. In type 1 diabetes, the immune system destroys insulin-producing cells, known as islet cells or beta cells, in the pancreas. Insulin is a hormone that allows cells to take in glucose (sugar used for energy) from the bloodstream. Without insulin, sugar and poisons build up in the blood, cells deteriorate, vital organs cannot function, and coma and death result. Even people who receive treatment with artificial insulin face blood sugar spikes that often lead to complications such as blindness, kidney failure, heart disease, limb amputations, and severe nerve pain.

Typical symptoms include excessive thirst, frequent urination, blurred vision, weight loss, weakness, fatigue, sweet-smelling breath, and sometimes mental confusion or mood changes. In a *Diabetes Health* article, teenage pop star Nick Jonas, who is one of the better-known celebrities with diabetes, reported "the usual symptoms: losing weight (fifteen pounds

Discoid lupus rashes are shown on a thirty-three-year-old female. It is a mild form of lupus, uncomfortable but not life-threatening.

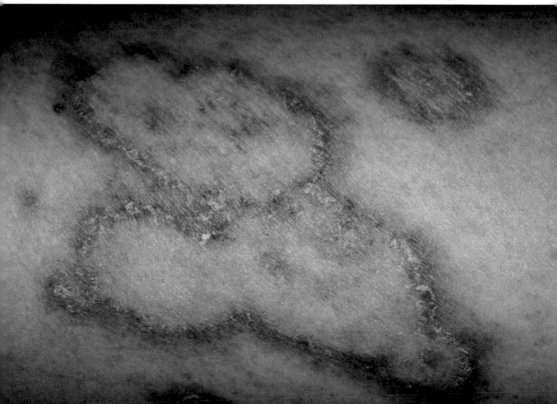

in two to three weeks), the bad attitude, being thirsty, going to the bathroom all the time. I had a terrible attitude, which was totally odd for me because I'm actually a nice person."[11] Jonas's blood sugar was a life-threatening 700mg/dl (milligrams per deciliter) when he became ill (normal is 70–120mg/dl).

While the diversity of affected body parts and symptoms in different autoimmune diseases prevented medical experts from recognizing the common autoimmune element for many years, doctors now know that similar biological processes underlie all of these disorders. Ongoing research into the causes of individual diseases and autoimmunity in general is yielding new insights into these processes every day.

CHAPTER TWO

What Causes Autoimmune Disorders?

Doctors have been baffled about the causes of autoimmune disorders since long before they knew an autoimmune attack was possible, and they have proposed and discarded a wide variety of theories. For example, the French doctor Jean Cruveilhier, who first described MS in 1835, believed a patient's inability to sweat caused the disease, since heat worsened patients' symptoms. Doctors now know that sweating or not sweating has nothing to do with causing MS. The renowned psychiatrist Sigmund Freud later proposed that emotional problems he called "female hysteria" caused MS; doctors no longer believe this either, though they acknowledge that stress can sometimes provoke or exacerbate the disease. Other doctors placed the blame on vitamin deficiencies, a high-fat diet, blood clots in the brain, and various vaccines. Modern experts still believe that some of these factors may contribute to MS, but they now know that a single cause is not responsible. Instead, complex interactions between biochemical, genetic, and environmental factors underlie MS and other autoimmune diseases.

The Basic Cause

The American Autoimmune Related Diseases Association (AARDA) explains that malfunctions during any phase of the immune process are the basic and immediate cause of all types of autoimmune diseases: "Autoimmune diseases occur when there is some interruption of the usual control process, allowing lymphocytes to avoid suppression, or when there is an alteration in some body tissue so that it is no longer recognized as 'self' and is thus attacked. The exact mechanisms causing these changes are not completely understood."[12]

Normally, the body works to promote self-tolerance (tolerating, or not attacking, its own cells) from the time when immune cells mature in the bone marrow or thymus. Studies have shown that before the cells leave these development sites, the body kills off most B cells and T cells that contain self-reactive receptors. Then, if some of these faulty cells escape into the

Artwork shows T cells (light-brown objects) attacking glial cells in an autoimmune disorder. T cells defend the body against infections.

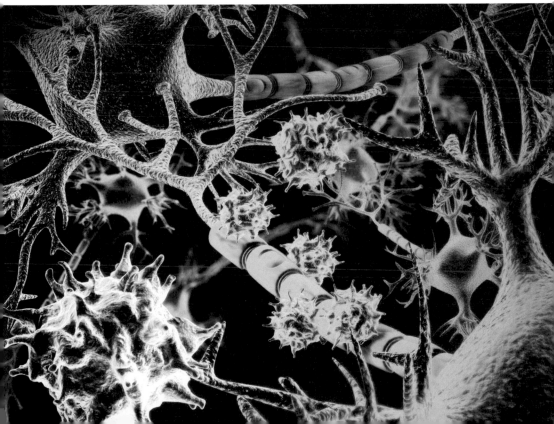

bloodstream, mechanisms exist that prevent activation signals from reaching them. But sometimes certain genetic or environmental factors disrupt these control mechanisms, and the self-reactive cells become activated anyway.

At other times, changes in regulatory T cells cause autoimmunity. In 2009 researchers at the University of California at San Francisco discovered that regulatory T cells that stop making a protein called FoxP3 cause diabetes in mice. The researchers explain:

> We believe the data suggest that not only can the regulatory T cells be dysfunctional and fail to suppress an autoimmune response, but they also can actively become disease-causing cells. Cells that appear to be protective regulatory T cells can turn into a different type of cell called a memory T cell, which attacks its molecular target instead of protecting the target from attack. The switch occurs when regulatory T cells stop making FoxP3.[13]

Other studies indicate that other body chemicals that affect T cells may also play a role. A 2010 NIAMS study, for example, found that the cytokines interleukin-6, interleukin-1-beta, and interleukin-23 stimulate the production of helper T cells that attack the self in mice. Another NIAMS study discovered that mice that lack a protein called furin in their T cells produce nonfunctional regulatory T cells and develop autoimmune diseases early in life. Whether these processes occur in humans remains to be seen.

Abnormally high or low numbers of different kinds of immune cells can also trigger autoimmunity. Doctors have discovered that MS patients have abnormally high numbers of helper and killer T cells and abnormally low numbers of regulatory T cells in their blood and cerebrospinal fluid (the liquid that surrounds the brain and spinal cord). Most people do not have any T cells at all in their cerebrospinal fluid because a mechanism called the blood-brain barrier prevents many cells and antigens from getting into the central nervous system. But somehow T cells manage to sneak past this barrier in people

Requirements for the Development of an Autoimmune Disease

The immune response of a genetically predisposed individual to an environmental pathogen, in association with certain defects, can lead to the development of an autoimmune disease. The importance of the single components may vary between individuals and diseases. However, the appearance of an autoimmune disorder requires the convergence of all three components.

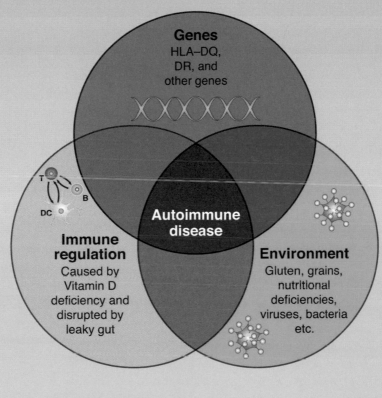

Taken from: *Nature Immunology* 2, 759–761/2001/dol:10.1038/ni0901-759.

with MS, and once in the nervous system, they proceed to attack the myelin on nerve cells.

Malfunctions in B cells can also lead to autoimmunity. Abnormal B cells or B cells that receive abnormal cytokine signals can produce autoantibodies (antibodies to the self) to specific body tissues or cells. Scientists are not sure whether these autoantibodies themselves attack body cells or whether they stimulate T cells to launch the attack in specific diseases.

Behind the Autoimmune Attack

While immune malfunctions are the immediate cause of auto-immune diseases, a combination of genetic and environmental factors in turn cause these malfunctions. Genes are the parts of DNA (deoxyribonucleic acid) molecules that pass heredi-tary information from parents to their offspring. They reside on wormlike bodies called chromosomes in the center of each cell. The sequence and chemical structure of genes encodes a set of instructions telling the cell how to operate.

Genetic information can either be received directly or be inherited as a predisposition. Examples of directly transmitted genetic traits are hair color and eye color. Such traits appear in the offspring regardless of environmental or biological events. When parents' genes have certain mutations, or abnormal changes in their chemical structure, these mutations can some-

A strand of DNA, which contains genetic instructions for the development and function of living organisms.

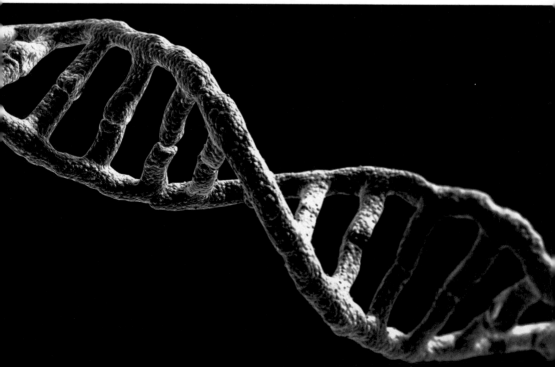

times be passed directly as well and can result in diseases like cystic fibrosis or sickle-cell anemia.

A genetic predisposition, in contrast, is an inherited tendency to develop certain traits or diseases and usually involves multiple genes or mutations. However, unless certain environmental or biological triggers are present, an individual with a predisposition is not likely to show that trait or get that disease. Doctors believe a genetic predisposition is involved in autoimmune diseases.

Evidence for Genetic Causes

Evidence that genetic factors play a role in causing autoimmune diseases comes from several types of studies. One type of study tracks the occurrence of these diseases in certain families. Such studies have shown that when one family member has an autoimmune disease, other family members are more likely than normal to develop one, though it may be a different autoimmune disease. Since close family members tend to share the same environment as well as have similar genes, scientists conduct other types of studies to assess the relative contributions of genetic and environmental factors.

These studies, which compare identical twins (who have identical genes) and fraternal twins (who do not have identical genes), show that identical twins both develop autoimmune disorders far more frequently than fraternal twins do. Such studies have led experts to conclude that genes account for about one-third of an individual's risk of developing an autoimmune disease.

The fact that some autoimmune diseases are more common in certain groups of people who share certain genetic traits also provides evidence for genetic involvement. For example, Caucasians get diabetes and MS far more often than people of other races do, and when African Americans and Hispanics get lupus, the disease tends to be more severe than it is in Caucasians, regardless of socioeconomic status. Scientists do not know, however, which genes underlie these racial disparities.

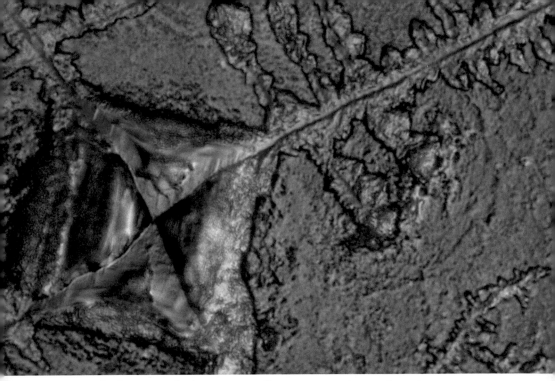

Magnified image of a human interferon, a protein produced in response to a viral infection. High levels of the cytokine interferon gamma in women may be the reason they are more susceptible to autoimmune disorders.

Women get many autoimmune diseases far more frequently than men do, and researchers are discovering clues as to why this happens. Scientists at the Mayo Clinic believe one factor may be that women are much more likely than men to have gene mutations that lead to high levels of the cytokine interferon gamma, which can activate an autoimmune attack. Sex hormones, which are regulated by genes, may also play a role in autoimmunity. Estrogen, the primary female hormone, can increase B cell, T cell, cytokine, and antibody production and activity. Pregnancy, which involves the production of several female hormones, can also affect the severity of certain autoimmune diseases. Many women with MS, for example, experience fewer flares during pregnancy than they do at other times. But pregnancy can worsen other autoimmune diseases like diabetes or lupus, and the precise role that hormones active during pregnancy play in these diseases is not yet well understood.

Other types of studies have identified specific genes in animals and humans that appear to be important in determining a susceptibility to autoimmunity. Over two hundred critical HLA genes on chromosome six (humans have forty-six chromosomes in each cell) and scores of other genes on other chromosomes may be involved in predisposing people to autoimmune diseases. For example, researchers have linked mutations in a gene called deformed epidermal autoregulatory factor to the development of diabetes in many people. They believe these mutations prevent the production of chemicals that would ordinarily destroy T cells, which attack islet cells.

Other gene mutations have been linked to other autoimmune diseases. A 2009 study at Stanford University identified two HLA gene mutations that cause the disease narcolepsy, which is characterized by irregular nighttime sleep and sudden lapses into sleep during the day. Prior to this study, no one knew for sure that narcolepsy was an autoimmune disease. But the investigators proved that the gene mutations cause the immune system to destroy cells that produce the hormone hypocretin, which is essential for normal sleep and wakefulness, and that the lack of hypocretin causes narcolepsy. "For a long time, people suspected narcolepsy had something to do with the immune system—that it was killing cells that produce hypocretin. But there hasn't been direct proof. Our discovery clearly shows narcolepsy is an autoimmune disease,"[14] explain the researchers.

Environmental Triggers

The key to a genetic susceptibility actually causing an autoimmune disease is one or more environmental or lifestyle triggers that activate the self-destructive switch. Scientists suspect but have not proved that certain triggers are responsible for many diseases. In other instances, though, convincing proof exists that certain factors are to blame.

A great deal of evidence suggests that certain viruses and bacteria may provoke autoimmunity, either soon after an infection or many years later. Experts believe this happens because these pathogens either alter body cells so the immune system perceives them as foreign, or because proteins in the microorganisms are chemically similar to a body part. In the latter case, after the immune system concludes its attack on the viruses or bacteria, it continues its assault on body tissues that resemble the foreign antigen. This has been proved to occur in some

An electron micrograph of the Epstein-Barr virus. Some scientists think the virus, which causes fevers, sore throat, and mononucleosis, is responsible for triggering lupus.

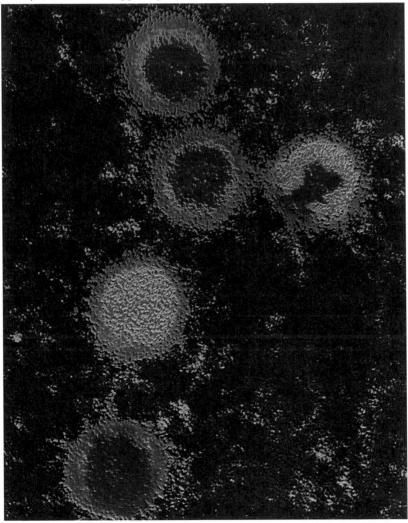

The Vaccine-Autoimmune Disease Link

There is no proof that the use of vaccines causes autoimmune disorders, but a perceived link between certain vaccines and autoimmunity in the last several decades has stirred controversy and conversation within the medical community. From 1976–1977, for example, doctors reported that an unusually large number of people developed Guillain-Barré syndrome after receiving a swine flu vaccination. No one proved that the vaccine caused Guillain-Barré, but public health officials in the United States stopped the widespread immunization program nonetheless.

Some studies have also suggested a link between the hepatitis B vaccine and diabetes and MS. In 1998 the Ministry of Health in France banned routine hepatitis B vaccinations for school-age children for this reason but later rescinded the ban because further studies failed to prove causality. A 2004 study reported in the journal *Neurology* found that people who received the hepatitis B vaccine were three times more likely to develop MS than those who did not receive it. A 2008 study reported in the *Open Pediatric Medical Journal* found that an unusually high number of children in Italy, France, and New Zealand developed diabetes two to four years after receiving the vaccine. The methodology and subsequent findings of these studies have been debated by experts, and similar studies led to mixed conclusions. As a result of the continuing debate over this vaccine's safety, some people have refused to be vaccinated or to allow their children to be vaccinated, despite the risk of contracting the hepatitis B virus. The CDC and other public health agencies, however, continue to recommend routine immunizations. In a statement on the link between hepatitis B vaccine and MS, for example, the CDC says, "The weight of the available evidence does not support the suggestion that hepatitis B vaccine causes or worsens MS."

Centers for Disease Control and Prevention. "FAQs About Hepatitis B Vaccine (Hep B) and Multiple Sclerosis." www.cdc.gov/vaccinesafety/vaccines/multiplesclerosis_and_hep_b.html.

people infected with the streptococcus bacterium that causes strep throat. These bacteria contain proteins that are similar to proteins found in heart cells, and doctors have found that when the immune system goes after these heart cells after it fights off a strep infection, the autoimmune disease rheumatic fever results.

In other instances, the role of certain viruses or bacteria is suspected but not proved. For example, many people with Guillain-Barré syndrome, a demyelinating disease character-ized by progressive paralysis of the limbs and internal organs, develop the disease about a month after having the flu, but no one has pinpointed exactly which flu virus is responsible or ex-plained why not everyone who develops Guillain-Barré had a previous flu infection. Studies also show a link between chick-enpox virus and diabetes, but no one has proved that this virus actually causes the disease. Some researchers have proposed that Epstein-Barr virus, which causes fever, sore throat, or mononucleosis, is responsible for triggering lupus years after an infection clears up, because the virus remains in the body and changes some body cells. Studies show that Epstein-Barr virus can activate B cells to produce autoantibodies in geneti-cally susceptible people, that 99 percent of children with lupus have the virus in their blood, and that laboratory animals given the virus often develop lupus. However, since most people are infected with this virus sometime during their lives and do not develop lupus, experts have concluded that although the virus can play a role in causing the disease, it is not the only neces-sary factor.

Vaccines

Some studies have suggested that there may be a connection between vaccines and the development of autoimmunity. Vaccines consist of inactivated viruses that stimulate the im-mune system to produce antibodies, which in turn prevent an individual from getting sick if he or she encounters the live vi-rus. While acknowledging that vaccines save millions of lives, some experts believe that some of the many vaccines routinely given to infants, children, and adults provoke autoimmunity in a manner similar to that in which live viruses and bacteria do—by changing body cells or being chemically similar to these cells. Other doctors hypothesize that the sheer number of vaccines given to modern babies and children (many receive about fifteen) overwhelm the immune system and are to blame for the rapid rise in the number of cases of autoimmune diseases over the past several decades. This topic is still controversial, however, as there is no scientific evidence that vaccines cause autoimmunity. Public health officials maintain that despite any possible links to autoimmunity, vaccines save many more lives than they endanger.

Lifestyle Factors

As with viruses and vaccines, no one is sure which, if any, lifestyle factors, such as diet, trigger autoimmunity, except in the case of celiac disease. Celiac is a condition in which eating foods (like wheat and rye) that contain a protein called gluten causes an immune assault on the small intestine, resulting in inflammation, pain, and an inability of the intestine to absorb

A patient with dermatomyositis displays the reddish rash on her hands that is often a sign of the disease.

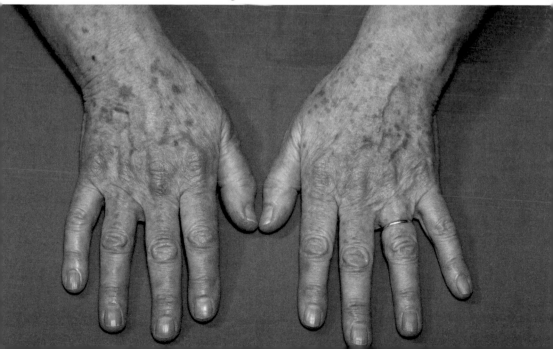

nutrients. Doctors know gluten causes celiac disease in genetically susceptible people because its symptoms go away when patients eliminate gluten from their diets.

Other dietary factors that may play a role in autoimmunity are iodine and vitamin D. Iodine is present in many foods, especially seafood, and studies on mice indicate that increasing the amount of iodine fed to genetically susceptible animals leads to autoimmune thyroiditis. No one knows if this occurs in humans. Vitamin D, which people get in some foods and from exposure to sunlight, is needed for normal immune function, and some doctors have proposed that people who have a vitamin D deficiency are more likely to develop autoimmune diseases. However, this has not been proved either.

The role that ultraviolet (UV) radiation from sunlight may play in autoimmunity is also unproved, but some evidence suggests that it may be involved. In 2009 scientists at the National Institutes of Health found that women who live in areas with high levels of UV radiation are more likely to develop the autoimmune disease dermatomyositis, which is characterized by a reddish-purple rash on the hands and eyelids. The researchers also found that higher UV levels increased the chances of women with the disease having anti-Mi-2 autoantibodies. Frederick Miller, one of the researchers, writes in a journal article that "although we have not shown a direct cause and effect link between UV levels and this particular autoimmune disease, this study confirms the association between UV levels and the frequency of dermatomyositis that we found in a previous investigation." Miller also points out that the study found no association between UV exposure and dermatomyositis in men: "It could be that inherent differences in how women and men respond to UV radiation may play a role in the development of certain autoimmune diseases."[15]

Other Lifestyle Links

Other lifestyle factors that have been implicated are physical trauma, hygiene, and stress. Doctors have reported that some people develop autoimmune diseases after a physical trauma,

Stress can provoke new autoimmune diseases and often worsens existing autoimmune diseases but researchers do not yet fully understand the process.

such as a blow to the eye, which causes fluids that are usually confined to the eyes to flow into the bloodstream. Experts have hypothesized that immune cells may not recognize these fluids as self, but no one has proved this theory.

The "Hygiene Hypothesis" put forth by several doctors states that the emphasis on being clean, along with successes in wiping out many infectious diseases in developed countries, may be responsible for the dramatic increases in autoimmune diseases in these places. Proponents of this theory believe the immune system may attack its own tissues because it is less occupied with protecting the body from invasion by foreign microorganisms. No one has proved this theory, and researchers continue to debate its merits, since cleanliness has been proved to save many lives by getting rid of nasty germs.

The role of stress in causing or worsening autoimmune disorders is much more widely accepted by medical experts. The author of *Women and Autoimmune Disease* explains:

> Stress can provoke new autoimmune disease and often worsens existing autoimmune disease in ways we do not fully understand. Many scientific studies have shown that immune cells drop in numbers when an animal or person is subjected to severe stress. I have personally known patients who suffer severe setbacks in their diseases when they are exposed to stresses such as a death in the family or a divorce.[16]

Tiffany was one young woman who developed lupus shortly after prolonged stress from her father's sudden death, her engagement to be married, and her fast-paced career in advertising. "My doctor told me that stress is definitely linked to lupus. . . . I'm not sure if stress was the sole trigger for my lupus, but it seems obvious to me that the two are connected."[17]

The Role of Chemicals

A great deal of evidence supports the theory that certain chemicals also trigger autoimmune diseases. Experts have proved that drugs like chlorpromazine, hydralazine, isoniazid, methyldopa, and penicillamine can cause a type of lupus called drug-induced lupus. When a patient discontinues taking these drugs, the lupus goes away. Drugs such as cephalosporin, penicillin, ibuprofen, interferon, levodopa, and procainamide are known to cause autoimmune hemolytic anemias, which are life-threatening diseases involving the destruction of red blood cells. Doctors believe these drugs stimulate the production of autoantibodies in susceptible people.

The Hygiene Hypothesis

The "Hygiene Hypothesis" put forth by some health experts states that cleanliness and the absence of many infectious diseases in developed countries may be causing increases in autoimmunity and allergies in these places. The World Health Organization points out that autoimmune diseases like diabetes and MS are rare in most underdeveloped countries in Africa and Asia, but when people from these areas migrate to industrialized places, rates of these diseases increase. Some experts believe this finding supports the "Hygiene Hypothesis," while others say exposure to factors (such as toxic chemicals and processed foods) other than cleanliness and fewer infections may be responsible.

Other experts point out that while good hygiene and cleanliness save many lives, they also wipe out many microorganisms that do no harm. An article in *ScienceNews Online* explains how this may affect the development of autoimmune diseases: "A growing number of scientists now suspect that stamping out these innocuous [harmless] organisms is weakening some parts of children's immune systems, allowing other parts to grow unchecked."

Siri Carpenter. "Modern Hygiene's Dirty Tricks." *ScienceNews*, August 14, 1999. www.sciencenews.org/pages/sn_arc99/8_14_99/bob2.htm.

The evidence linking environmental chemicals to autoimmunity is not as strong as that for drugs but does suggest that these substances play a role. One class of substances that researchers suspect is polybrominated diphenyl ethers (PBDEs), which are flame retardants added to clothing, car and airplane seats, walls, plastics, and electronic products to reduce the risk of burning. PBDEs tend to rapidly degrade and escape into the air, water, soil, and food and dust in homes. People can then inhale or ingest these chemicals, and studies have found that Americans have high levels of PBDEs in their blood and breast milk. The EPA banned two particularly dangerous PBDEs called penta-BDEs and octa-BDEs, but similar chemicals are still widely used. The CDC issued a statement saying, "Preliminary evidence suggests that high concentrations of PBDE's may cause neurochemical alterations and affect the immune system in animals."[18]

Perfluorooctanoic acid (PFOA) used in nonstick cookware, car parts, clothing, dishes, and furniture; silica, found in rocks, sand, and concrete; the cleaning solvent trichloroethylene (TCE); polychlorinated biphenyls (PCBs) used in plastics, electrical equipment, insulation, glues, and paints; dioxins used in preservatives and bleaches and released in car and truck fumes; pesticides used to kill bugs; and herbicides in weed killers are other chemicals linked to autoimmune diseases. For example, studies have shown that farmers regularly exposed to pesticides are more likely than other people to have high levels of autoantibodies in their blood, and all the mice exposed to low levels of the pesticide methoxychlor in one experiment developed lupus. Other research has shown that when female rats are exposed to dioxin during pregnancy, their offspring are highly likely to develop autoimmune diseases after birth. One study reported in 2009 found that exposure to dioxins before birth impaired the ability of baby mice to produce regulatory T cells and also led to abnormal cytokines. Other research has found that dioxin causes the thymus, where T cells mature, to shrink in people, thereby decreasing the number of regulatory T cells in the body.

Heavy Metals

Another type of suspected environmental trigger is heavy metals like gold, silver, and, particularly, lead and mercury. Studies have linked lead to a variety of diseases in children, and researchers have proved that it alters the immune system in laboratory animals, so it may play a role in human autoimmunity as well, though there is as yet no proof.

A 2006 study in Taiwan found that mercury exposure led to the destruction of islet cells in mice, and other studies indicate that mercury causes an overproduction of lymphocytes and inflammatory cytokines in these animals. In 2009 researchers at the Johns Hopkins Bloomberg School of Public Health found that miners exposed to mercury in their work showed much higher levels of autoantibodies and cytokines that cause inflammation than did other miners. "This study provides further

Studies have linked heavy metals like gold, silver, lead, and mercury to a variety of childhood autoimmune disorders.

evidence that mercury exposure may lead to autoimmune dys-function and systemic inflammation,"[19] write the researchers.

Since scientists have not yet proved that many suspected environmental toxins actually cause autoimmune disorders, much research that seeks to clearly understand and define the role they play is currently under way. Research into the genetic and biochemical causes continues as well, in the hope that a better understanding of these processes will lead to improved methods of treatment or even prevention.

CHAPTER THREE

Diagnosis and Treatment

As with the causes of autoimmune disorders, doctors still have a great deal to learn about their diagnosis and treatment. Diagnosing some diseases is especially difficult, and treatments can be ineffective or have dangerous side effects.

A variety of medical specialists can diagnose and treat these disorders. Sometimes general practitioners or internists who deal with overall health do this, but many patients consult specialists who focus on specific organs or body systems. Someone who suspects they have or has rheumatoid arthritis, for example, is likely to consult a rheumatologist, who specializes in the joints. A patient with MS will probably see a neurologist, who focuses on the nervous system.

Doctors initially take a medical history, which details symptoms, family history of certain diseases, past surgeries, and lifestyle habits such as diet, exercise, and smoking. Then the physician performs a physical examination to check temperature, heart rate, blood pressure, rashes, muscle strength, ability to walk, and tenderness throughout the body. The medical history and physical exam may offer clues about what may be wrong, but further tests are needed to confirm any suspicions and pinpoint a specific disease. These tests may consist of blood and urine tests, imaging studies, organ biopsies (where the doctor uses a hollow needle to extract a

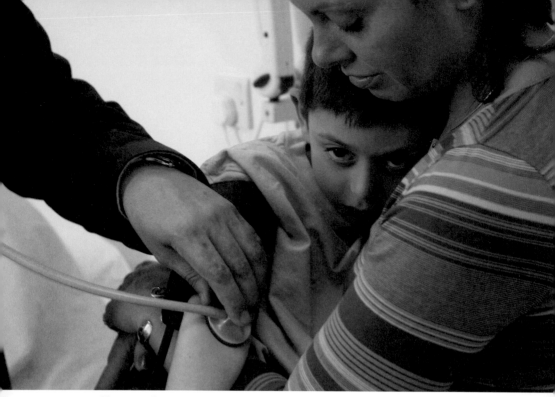

In an effort to diagnose an autoimmune disorder, family medical history is considered. The physician performs a physical examination to check temperature, heart rate, blood pressure, rashes, and tenderness throughout the body.

small piece of tissue and examines the sample under a microscope), and nerve conduction tests to ascertain the presence of a neurological disease.

Not all suspected diseases require all these tests. For example, a blood test that measures blood sugar level is all that is needed to diagnose diabetes. If an individual's blood sugar is higher than 126mg/dl after the person has not eaten for at least eight hours or after he or she drinks a sugary beverage, a doctor can diagnose the disease. Diabetes is also easy to diagnose because the symptoms are specific to the disease.

Difficulties in Diagnosis

Most other autoimmune disorders are much more difficult to diagnose, and sometimes an individual will not receive an accurate diagnosis for many years because symptoms and laboratory test results are not specific to any one disease. The

Sjogren's Syndrome Foundation, for instance, says, "On average it takes nearly seven years to receive a diagnosis of Sjogren's syndrome."[20] In general, about half of all people who have one or more autoimmune diseases report that they failed to receive a diagnosis for an average of five years.

The American Autoimmune Related Diseases Association (AARDA) explains that another factor that plays a role in delaying diagnosis is that many doctors do not take some patients, particularly women, seriously when they complain of certain symptoms, and indeed label them "chronic complainers" or "hypochondriacs" who are imagining that they are sick. One AARDA study found that 45 percent of women with autoimmune diseases were labeled in this manner during the early stages of their illnesses.

In many such cases, says AARDA,

> Victims face problems not only because physicians don't think of autoimmunity, but also because of who they are, namely women in the childbearing years. As a rule, this is a time in a woman's life when she looks healthy, though looks can be deceiving. . . . A woman's symptoms are likely to be vague in the beginning, with a tendency to come and go, and hard to describe accurately. In a typical scenario, she is often shunted from specialist to specialist and forced to undergo a battery of tests and procedures before a correct diagnosis is made.[21]

Lisa, for example, was finally diagnosed with rheumatoid arthritis after several years of having doctors tell her she was imagining her symptoms: "I bounced from doctor to doctor with everyone telling me I was too young to have the symptoms I was having. The doctors were resistant to testing me. I even went to one with severe swelling in my hands and feet and he *still* told me it was all in my head."[22]

Tests for Autoimmunity

When a doctor does suspect that a patient has some sort of autoimmune disease, he or she will generally order several types of blood tests in addition to the blood cell counts and other routine tests that can rule out other diseases. The most common tests are erythrocyte sedimentation rate (ESR), c-reactive protein (CRP), complement, and antinuclear antibody (ANA). ESR measures how fast erythrocytes (red blood cells) separate from blood plasma (the liquid part of blood) in a test tube. If inflammation in the body is present, certain proteins attach to erythrocytes and cause them to stick together. They then become heavier and drop away from plasma more quickly than they normally would. An ESR test, however, only indicates whether inflammation exists but does not specify the source.

The liver produces CRP, and levels of this protein rise when a person has inflammation throughout the body. This test can thus be useful in alerting a doctor to a non-organ-specific au-

Equipment used to measure the erythrocyte sedimentation rate (ESR). The ESR measures how fast red blood cells separate from blood plasma in a test tube.

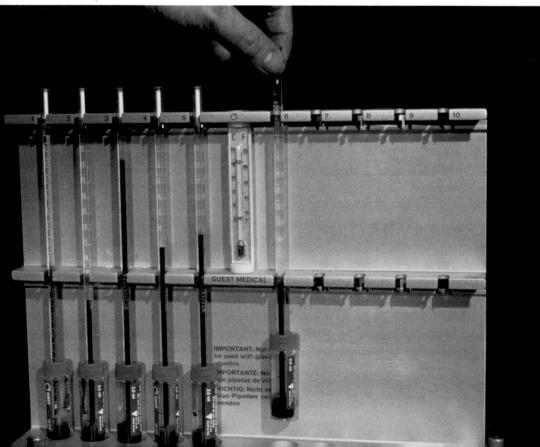

toimmune disease. But, for unknown reasons, CRP is rarely elevated in people with rheumatoid arthritis and lupus, so a normal CRP reading does not necessarily mean an individual does not have these diseases.

Testing for complement proteins is another nonspecific test that can reveal immune activity, but it does not pinpoint which, if any, autoimmune disease is present. An ANA test, though, is a much more conclusive indicator of autoimmunity. The ANA test reveals whether significant numbers of antibodies to the patient's own DNA are present. A positive ANA usually, but not always, indicates that a person has some sort of autoimmune disease. Sometimes various qualities seen in the test, such as patterns in which the cell nucleus, or center, stains with a dye, can give clues as to which autoimmune disease is involved. But not all people with a positive ANA have an autoimmune disorder; this is known as a false positive. In other cases, a person with a positive ANA may not yet have symptoms of any disease, but a doctor can warn the individual that he or she may develop symptoms in the future.

Tests for Specific Autoimmune Diseases

If an ANA and other blood tests reveal the presence of inflammation and/or autoimmunity, doctors often will order further tests that measure specific autoantibodies to find out which disease a person has. There are many, many types of autoantibodies, and some are present in more than one disease. Typical autoantibodies found in lupus patients, for example, are anti-DNA, anti-Smith (anti-Sm), and anti-ribonucleoprotein (anti-RNP). Anti-DNA antibodies are seen in many autoimmune diseases, and anti-RNP is seen in mixed connective tissue diseases as well as in lupus. Anti-Sm is more specific to lupus and is so named for Stephanie Smith, the first lupus patient in whom it was found.

In addition to using these autoantibody tests to diagnose lupus, doctors may also perform a skin or kidney biopsy to check for certain types of inflammation typically seen in the disease. Then, based on symptoms, biopsy results, and blood tests, they

The ANA Test

The antinuclear antibody (ANA) test is widely used to determine whether an individual has an autoimmune disease. Results can also give doctors clues about which disease is present. Technicians assess whether a blood sample is ANA positive by diluting the blood with saline solution and counting the number of times the sample must be diluted before antinuclear antibodies are no longer detectable. This measurement is called a titer. A titer of 1:40, for example, means ANA can no longer be detected after forty dilutions. Experts consider a titer of 1:80 or lower to be a negative ANA reading (even people who do not have an autoimmune disease can have low levels of ANA in their blood). Those with a titer greater than 1:80 are likely to have an autoimmune disorder.

After performing a titer, technicians stain the blood cells with special dyes and examine the resulting staining patterns under a microscope. Different patterns can reveal the presence of different autoantibodies associated with certain autoimmune diseases. For instance, a homogenous pattern, characterized by the cells' entire nucleus, or center, absorbing the dye, often appears when lupus autoantibodies are present. A speckled pattern appears when discrete areas in the nucleus absorb dye and may indicate Sjogren's syndrome, scleroderma, polymyositis, rheumatoid arthritis, or mixed connective tissue disease. Further chemical tests are needed in such cases to confirm precisely which autoantibodies and which disease exist. Other staining patterns include rim, nucleolar, and centromere.

can diagnose the disease based on American College of Rheumatology criteria stating that a diagnosis of lupus requires at least four out of eleven symptoms and test results.

Diagnosing other autoimmune diseases may require other types of tests. For example, a definitive diagnosis of MS requires MRI (magnetic resonance imaging) tests that reveal plaques in the nervous system. Diagnosing Sjogren's syndrome involves performing blood tests for disease-specific SS-A and SS-B autoantibodies, along with eye tests to measure tear production and view dry spots as well as tests on the salivary glands in the mouth to assess inflammation and lack of saliva production.

After the Diagnosis

After a doctor diagnoses an autoimmune disease, treatment, if needed and available, can begin. Effective treatments are thus far available for only about 10 percent of the known autoimmune diseases. No cures exist for any autoimmune diseases yet, so treatment must usually continue for the rest of a person's life.

Treatment for some diseases, such as diabetes, must start immediately or the patient will die. In other diseases like rheumatoid arthritis or MS, starting treatment may be less urgent, and sometimes patients elect to wait and see how symptoms progress before starting on medications that can have dangerous side effects. More and more doctors, however, are emphasizing that it is important to begin treatment right away even in these diseases, since modern drugs can often slow the progression of the disease and prevent some disabling consequences.

According to AARDA, "Of first importance in treating any autoimmune disease is the correction of any major deficiencies. Second in importance is diminishing the activity of the immune system."[23] For some diseases, such as celiac disease or drug-induced lupus, treatment involves only removing known disease triggers (gluten or certain drugs, respectively). For other disorders, treatment for specific symptoms like pain or muscle spasms or for complications may be needed as well as disease-altering therapy.

Examples of diseases that require correcting deficiencies are diabetes, hemolytic anemias, and Sjogren's syndrome. People with type 1 diabetes must inject fast-acting and slow-acting insulins several times each day or receive insulin infusions through an insulin pump attached to tubing under the skin. They must also stick their fingers multiple times each day to test their blood sugar levels using a device called a glucose monitor, and they must pay careful attention to their diet and exercise to keep blood sugar levels as normal as possible. Insulin injections, food intake, and exercise must be in balance to prevent blood sugars from becoming dangerously high or low. If someone with diabetes exercises more than usual, for example, his or her blood

Many diabetics must inject insulin several times each day or receive insulin infusions through an insulin pump attached to tubing under the skin.

sugar may drop to dangerously low levels unless he or she eats an extra snack or injects less insulin than normal. If he or she eats too much, an extra injection of fast-acting insulin may be needed. Cell damage or even coma and death can result from blood sugar that becomes too low or too high.

Treating hemolytic anemias, which involve the destruction of red blood cells, requires replacing lost red blood cells with blood transfusions in the hospital, as well as sometimes keeping the patient alive with life-saving machines and medications if life-threatening complications result from the disease. People with Sjogren's often need over-the-counter or prescription moisturizing eye drops or gels, such as Restasis® or Lacrisert®; dry mouth medications like Evoxac® or Numoisyn™; and frequent applications of rich skin creams to alleviate very dry skin. Some patients also benefit from drugs called immunosuppressives, which diminish the immune attack, but in most cases these drugs are not effective for treating this disease.

Immunosuppresives
Drugs that suppress the immune system, however, are the mainstay of treatment for many other autoimmune disorders. While these medications often help alleviate symptoms or even slow progression of certain diseases, they are also dangerous because suppressing immunity means the body cannot fight infections and cancers. Some of the newer immunosuppressives target specific immune cells or chemicals in an attempt to inhibit only those parts of the immune system that are contributing to autoimmunity, but thus far even these drugs result in a reduced overall ability to fight infections and cancers.

The most commonly used immunosuppressives for alleviating symptoms are corticosteroids such as prednisone. Cortisol is a naturally occurring steroid produced by the adrenal glands. It decreases inflammation and thus helps alleviate pain and swelling. Doctors prescribe synthetic corticosteroids, which can be taken orally or by injection or intravenous infusion, to treat flare-ups in diseases like MS, lupus, and rheumatoid arthritis. These drugs act by blocking lymphocytes and inflammatory chemicals called prostaglandins. But in addition to impairing an individual's ability to fight infections, corticosteroids can also cause weight gain, stomach ulcers, mood swings, and high blood sugar levels. Thus, doctors often prescribe high doses to initially treat a disease flare-up, but then gradually reduce the dosage and eventually discontinue the drugs for as long as possible to avoid these side effects.

For some patients, drugs called nonsteroidal anti-inflammatory drugs (NSAIDS), such as aspirin, ibuprofen, and naproxen, or other pain medicines such as acetaminophen or prescription narcotic painkillers work well, and in these cases people can use these medications instead of corticosteroids. But these drugs can also have side effects, such as liver and kidney damage and gastrointestinal bleeding, so they must also be used carefully.

Another type of immunosuppressive treatment is called intravenous immunoglobin therapy. Here, immunoglobins, or antibodies, taken from the blood of many people are sterilized and infused into a patient through an intravenous tube over several hours. Experts are not sure how and why this treatment works but believe that some antibodies decrease inflammation by blocking autoantibodies and by breaking down immune complexes. However, this treatment can cost several thousand dollars and only gives temporary results, so it is not used as often as corticosteroids, which cost about two dollars per pill.

Disease-Modifying Drugs

While corticosteroids and pain medications can alleviate symptoms, they do nothing to alter the progression of autoimmune diseases, and many patients must also take disease-modifying immunosuppressives to try to reduce ongoing damage and disability. The type of disease-modifying drugs used depends on the particular disease. Doctors often prescribe injectable synthetic interferon beta, for example, to reduce the frequency and severity of flare-ups and to diminish plaques in people with MS. Synthetic interferon beta is a human-made form of the naturally occurring cytokine. It can have unpleasant side

Rituximab has been used to treat rheumatoid arthritis because it destroys B cells.

effects such as swelling and pain at the injection site, depression, fever, and aches and pains, and does not help all patients.

Other disease-modifying drugs used to treat MS are glatiramer acetate, which resembles myelin and thus fools the immune system into attacking it instead of the person's myelin, and natalizumab, which prevents T cells from crossing the blood-brain barrier. Glatiramer acetate, however, does not help as many patients as interferon beta does, and natalizumab can cause a fatal brain infection, so it is not used unless nothing else works.

Natalizumab is one of a new class of injectable drugs called biologic agents. These drugs are designed to target specific cells or body chemicals. Some biologic agents whose names end with "mab" are monoclonal antibodies, which scientists make by cloning a single antibody.

Different biologics target different cells or chemicals. Rituximab, for example, which is used to treat rheumatoid arthritis, destroys B cells. Several others—adalimumab, golimomab, infliximab, and etanercept—suppress the cytokine called tumor necrosis factor (TNF) and are known as TNF inhibitors. Although TNF inhibitors have helped induce remissions in many people with diseases like rheumatoid arthritis and Crohn's disease who were not helped by other treatments, they place patients at four to five times the normal risk for serious infections like pneumonia, tuberculosis, and bladder infections, increase the risk of cancers like lymphoma, and can decrease white blood cell and platelet counts to dangerously low levels. Many patients also cannot afford these drugs, which can cost about two thousand dollars per month. Still, many experts believe TNF inhibitors have done more good than harm. As rheumatologist Daniel Furst of the University of California at Los Angeles stated in an AARDA publication, "I can't emphasize enough how important these drugs have been to patients. Previously, we did not even talk about remission. Now, although there is a lot of controversy about what remission actually means, by some definitions about 30 to 50 percent of patients taking these drugs go into remission. This was unheard of 15 years ago. These drugs are having a very positive effect."[24]

Many patients, particularly those with rheumatoid arthritis, take biologics in combination with other medications called disease-modifying antirheumatic drugs (DMARDS). DMARDS can take up to a month to start showing positive effects but end up reducing inflammation and joint damage over the long term for many patients. They are much less costly than biologics; generally one to four dollars per pill, depending on the drug. They can have serious side effects, though, and pregnant

The Development of TNF-Alpha Inhibitors

Ravinder Maini and Marc Feldmann of the Kennedy Institute of Rheumatology at Imperial College London did much of the pioneering work in developing the first TNF-alpha inhibitors. Maini, who was born in India and educated in England, and Feldmann, who was born and educated in Australia, began their collaborative research on cytokines and antibodies in the 1980s. After identifying TNF-alpha as an important inflammatory cytokine, they went on to discover that people with autoimmune diseases cannot remove or inhibit this chemical, so inflammation continues indefinitely. The team then experimented with various compounds to try to block TNF-alpha from acting on immune cells. They succeeded in synthesizing a monoclonal antibody called infliximab, and in 1992 and 1993 demonstrated that it was effective in diminishing symptoms in patients with rheumatoid arthritis. This was the first biologic drug that proved to be successful in treating a chronic disease, and the discovery led to the development of other targeted biologics for use in many other disorders.

Maini and Feldmann have received many awards, including the Albert Lasker Clinical Medical Research Award and the Dr. Paul Janssen Award for Biomedical Research, for their contributions to enhancing the understanding of the immune system and for directly benefiting patients who suffer from autoimmune diseases.

women can never take them because they cause severe damage to a fetus.

Common DMARDS include methotrexate, hydroxychloroquine, leflunomide, and cyclosporine. Methotrexate was strictly used as a cancer drug for many years. Then, doctors discovered it reduced inflammation and bone damage in people with arthritis. Since the drug can have serious side effects, such as mouth sores, nausea, vomiting, fever, infection, and liver and bone marrow damage, doctors try to prescribe low doses and carefully monitor patients who take it.

Hydroxychloroquine is usually used to treat malaria but has been found to reduce inflammation in people with arthritis, lupus, and other autoimmune diseases as well. Doctors are not sure how it works to reduce inflammation. It has fewer side effects than most DMARDS but can damage the eyes if taken for long periods of time.

Leflunomide also inhibits inflammation but can have numerous side effects like rashes, hair loss, liver damage, nausea, diarrhea, weight loss, and abdominal pain. It operates by inhibiting the synthesis of an enzyme called dihydroorotate dehydrogenase, and this results in the immune system producing fewer lymphocytes.

Cyclosporine was originally developed to prevent rejection of transplanted organs and is now used to treat many autoimmune disorders. It inhibits the inflammatory cytokine interleukin-2, and can have serious side effects like infection, high blood pressure, kidney disease, nausea, vomiting, and diarrhea, so many doctors hesitate to prescribe it unless other drugs are ineffective.

Treatment Challenges and Additional Methods

Since many drugs like corticosteroids, biologics, and DMARDS can have such serious side effects, doctors and patients must carefully weigh their risks against benefits for an individual. If a patient has more than one autoimmune disease, this can make treatment decisions especially challenging. The drugs used to treat one disease may either interact adversely with drugs used to treat another disease, or certain drugs that benefit one disease may worsen another. For example, people with diabetes should not take corticosteroids or other immunosuppressives because these medications raise blood sugar and can impair an already challenged ability to fight infections. If a patient also has MS, arthritis, or another disease that requires these drugs, a physician will try to prescribe very low doses or even different drugs if they are available and effective.

Besides having to optimize drug treatments for each patient, doctors may also have to refer people with one or more autoimmune diseases to other specialists for additional forms of treatment. Many people need psychotherapy for the depression that often goes along with having a chronic disease. Some need physical therapy that helps them stretch their muscles or perform exercises to regain or retain motion when impaired nerves or joints make movement difficult. Others need occupational therapy for assistance with everyday activities like eating and dressing. Physical and occupational therapists can recommend assistive devices like wheelchairs, canes, walkers, or special eating utensils to make it easier for someone to get around and perform certain tasks.

Alternative Treatments

Because many existing treatments are ineffective, expensive, have dangerous side effects, and do not cure autoimmune diseases, many patients seek alternative or complementary therapies. Some of these therapies are helpful, but many are not scientifically proven to be beneficial, and many are not accepted by mainstream medical doctors. Some are even harmful.

Complementary therapy is used in conjunction with conventional treatment, and alternative therapies are used instead of conventional treatments. Both may involve special diets, herbal or vitamin supplements, massage, acupuncture, or other options. Most experts say some of these therapies are safe and effective as complementary treatments but that using them instead of conventional treatment can be extremely dangerous and allow a disease to progress unchecked.

Acupuncture is one therapy that has been proved to be safe and effective as a complementary treatment when administered by a licensed doctor. It involves the doctor placing fine needles at certain points on the skin to relieve pain and other symptoms and is especially effective for alleviating pain. In contrast, other therapies such as special diets rarely produce

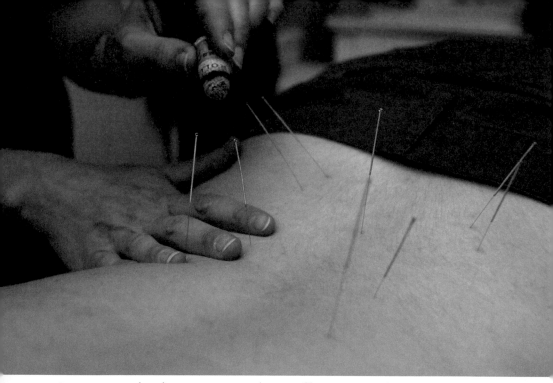

Acupuncture has been proven to be an effective complementary treatment for some autoimmune disorders.

results, and still others such as herbs may be harmful. As autoimmune disease expert Robert Lahita explains in *Women and Autoimmune Disease*, "Most herbal preparations stimulate immune function, and that is in direct opposition to our therapeutic goal for autoimmune diseases. No one should ever use an herb supplement after a diagnosis of an autoimmune disease."[25]

A woman named Bea, who had idiopathic thrombocytopenic purpura, a disease in which the immune system destroys blood platelets needed for clotting, died after using herbs she bought from an herbalist instead of following her doctor's advice, and many other patients have died or suffered as well. Other controversial alternative treatments touted for various autoimmune disorders are bee venom, snake venom, magnets, special exercises, and chelation (an infusion of chemicals that supposedly remove toxins and metals from the blood).

Many alternative medicine practitioners and supplement manufacturers make dramatic claims about secret or miracle cures, and many patients are lured by these claims and even spend thousands of dollars on bogus scams. One woman with MS, for example, spent one hundred thousand dollars on a phony exercise cure touted by a doctor (who later lost his medical license), and her physical condition deteriorated rapidly. In an article for the National Multiple Sclerosis Society, she told other patients,

> I want to warn you that MS can make you desperate, and desperation makes you vulnerable—an easy target for snake-oil salesmen selling false hope and phony cures. I know. I was a victim. . . . Within seven months, my condition deteriorated. . . . I had to quit my job, I needed 24-hour nursing care, and I now use a wheelchair full-time. While there are honest and honorable people who offer alternative medical treatments, there are too many charlatans who will prey on your desperation.[26]

One controversial treatment for various autoimmune disorders is bee sting therapy, known as apitherapy.

Experts recommend that patients especially avoid any alternative treatments that are advertised online, on television and radio, in newspapers or magazines in advertisements disguised as articles, or even in books written by doctors if the advertisers tout a cure, miracle, or secret treatment; if upfront payment is required and a money-back guarantee not offered; and if testimonials from so-called satisfied people are given.

However, until scientists succeed in developing legitimate cures and less dangerous treatments for autoimmune diseases, many patients will try unproved remedies in an attempt to make their lives with these diseases easier.

CHAPTER FOUR

Living with Autoimmune Disorders

Living with the physical and emotional challenges presented by autoimmune disorders can be frightening and life changing, especially since these diseases often begin during childhood, adolescence, or young adulthood, when people do not expect to have to deal with a chronic illness. According to NIAID, "Since cures are not yet available . . . patients face a lifetime of illness and treatment."[27]

People with any sort of chronic disease are more likely than normal to experience ongoing depression, which is characterized by feelings of hopelessness and helplessness, sleep problems, and loss of interest in activities. But many patients move beyond the initial shock and depression they feel after diagnosis and manage to accept and deal with their condition, despite the constant doctor visits, pain, medications, and, in some cases, hospitalizations. AARDA explains:

> When you are diagnosed with a serious chronic autoimmune disease, it is normal to question your well-being and your mental ability to cope with the life changes that are part of living successfully with any serious chronic illness. Typically, newly diagnosed patients feel the "anger, denial,

bargaining, depression and acceptance" cycle identified by [Elisabeth] Kübler-Ross as a response to coping with significant loss and major life changes.[28]

When teenage pop star Nick Jonas was diagnosed with diabetes at age fourteen, he was overwhelmed at first. "For someone who had no bad medical history ever, to suddenly have the shock of diabetes was a bit overwhelming in itself, and then I had to learn all about it, learn all these things in such a short period of time. I also wondered if I could continue making music,"[29] he said in an article in *Diabetes Health*. But with support from his family and friends, Jonas learned to accept his situation and to continue with his career, albeit with important lifestyle modifications.

Nick Jonas of the Jonas Brothers teen band talks to the press about living with juvenile diabetes.

A Frustrating Process

Sometimes emotional difficulties and uncertainties occur before diagnosis, especially when doctors fail to believe anything is wrong with a patient. Lisa, who was frustrated by not being diagnosed with rheumatoid arthritis for several years after her symptoms started, was both relieved and angry when she finally received her diagnosis:

> I finally found a rheumatologist who was willing to do some tests and conduct a thorough history, as well as talk about what was going on in my life. I felt a great sense of relief to finally have a diagnosis. When you hurt for years and don't get the treatment you need—or even get listened to—finally having a diagnosis is very freeing. I was also very angry because it shouldn't have taken that long.[30]

Even after diagnosis, the fact that oftentimes the pain and disability from certain diseases are not visible to others can be frustrating for patients when family members, coworkers, or friends think the patient is not really sick. Kathleen, who suffers from several autoimmune diseases, remarks, "People don't see what lies behind the scenes in most autoimmune diseases. Because we go through ups and downs, you might see us on a good day, between severe flares, when we seem to be perfectly fine. You don't know that we've just spent six weeks in hell."[31]

Sudden Changes

Another frustrating part of living with autoimmune diseases is that they can literally change an individual's life overnight. Patients may suddenly have to stop doing things they enjoy, stop working, stop driving, or even become unable to care for themselves. Jan, who greatly enjoyed taking long bicycle rides with her husband, could no longer do that after antiphospholipid syndrome, which involves an attack on proteins that normally prevent blood from clotting too much, nearly killed her. Many patients have to stop working, either temporarily or permanently, and this can result in financial difficulties as well

Coping with an Autoimmune Disease

The American Autoimmune Related Diseases Association recommends some ways of coping with an autoimmune disorder:

• Understand your illness and the treatment plan established by your physician. Ask questions of your doctor about your particular condition, especially what changes and symptoms you can expect to encounter.

• Let your doctor know if some new symptom is occurring. Persons with chronic illness often feel that their doctors are going to think they are chronic complainers if they are honest about how they are feeling. It is much better to discuss what is going on and how it might be treated than to worry about what the doctor will think.

• Fatigue may accompany many of the autoimmune diseases. Learning how to pace your activity level can put you in control of your illness.

• Use "I" messages with others. If you are not feeling well, say "I'm not feeling well and I could really use your support."

• Give yourself and your family time to adjust. Nobody adjusts overnight to something that may significantly impact the rest of his or her life.

• Understand that you did nothing to cause your illness and that life is not always fair. Bad things do happen to almost everyone at sometime in a lifetime. It is how we deal with these life changes that makes the difference between a life of coping and a life of moping.

American Autoimmune Related Diseases Association. "Coping with Autoimmunity." www.aarda.org/coping.php.

as in feelings of helplessness and loss. In some cases, people can shift to a less physically demanding job, telecommute, or work reduced hours, but not all jobs allow this. The Americans with Disabilities Act requires employers to make reasonable accommodations for employees with certain disabilities, but this is not always possible if the person can no longer do his or her job. Some patients are able to launch an entirely new career; Amy, for example, who had to stop teaching because of severe lupus, decided to start writing books. Although the lupus prevented her from typing on a computer, she was able

People with MS or lupus have ongoing fatigue and must set aside time to rest each day.

to obtain special software and hardware that allowed her to dictate her stories into the computer. She began publishing history books and novels for children.

Other people suddenly lose the ability to do much of anything. A young woman named Helen writes, "For awhile I had to rely totally on my family; my husband bathed me, washed my hair, cut up my food and fed me. I take a lot of medication and wonder what it's like to feel normal, never tired, no pain and a fully alert mind."[32]

For others, normal activities may continue with restrictions. Travel, for instance, may become challenging but doable with preplanning for people with diabetes, who must keep their insulin refrigerated or cool in an insulated bag with an ice pack. This requires careful planning to make sure the ice pack can be refrozen each day in a hotel room refrigerator or other place. In addition, people with diabetes must continue a regular schedule of insulin injections, blood tests, and meals, and this can be difficult while on a plane, in a car, or when sightseeing.

Those with diseases like MS or lupus, which involve ongoing fatigue, must set aside time to rest each day, even on vacation. This can be frustrating or make a patient feel left out if he or she must take a nap while family members are out exploring.

Special Problems for Women

Autoimmune disorders can also impact the lives of women and children in unique ways. Because many of these diseases strike women in their childbearing years, this can affect their ability to have or care for children. Doctors often advise women with some diseases, particularly those that affect multiple organs, not to risk pregnancy because of potential damage to the mother and fetus. Women with antiphospholipid syndrome, for example, are generally advised that pregnancy would increase the risk of serious blood clots and kidney disease. Those with scleroderma, which affects connective tissue throughout the body, are also at high risk for complications or death if they become pregnant.

In some cases, medications that a woman has to take, such as DMARDS, can cause birth defects, so pregnancy is not an

Doctors often recommend that women with some autoimmune disorders not risk pregnancy because of potential damage to the fetus and mother.

option. But many women who do not take such drugs, or who have other diseases that are well controlled, can safely become pregnant and deliver a healthy baby as long as they and the doctor are prepared to deal with the complications that may result from a high-risk pregnancy. Many women with well-controlled diabetes, for example, have successful pregnancies, though they must carefully monitor weight gain and blood sugar levels because the risk of miscarriage and large babies is high.

Women with autoimmune diseases who already have children may have difficulty caring for them when flares or complications occur. Lisa, who has rheumatoid arthritis, writes, "You miss out on a lot when you are in so much pain. I wasn't able to do as much with my kids when they were younger. I couldn't attend sporting events during bad flare-ups. Not being able to pick up the kids really bothered me. I could sit down and they could crawl in my lap, but being a mom and not being able to pick up my kids was tough."[33]

Special Challenges for Children and Teens

Children and teens with autoimmune diseases also face special challenges. "Children can feel hurt by an illness that isn't their fault, blame parents for the illness, engage in self-pity or become angry because of restrictions on activities. They may also resent other children who do not have the disease, including their brothers and sisters,"[34] explains the Arthritis Foundation.

Jessica, who was diagnosed with diabetes at age sixteen, felt left out and resented the daily treatments the disease required: "When I heard what was involved in treating diabetes—injecting myself twice daily with insulin, testing my blood, monitoring my diet—I was more upset than I've ever been. To make matters worse, I couldn't have any candy that Halloween and was stuck at home handing out candy to trick-or-treaters."[35]

The authors of *The Encyclopedia of Autoimmune Disorders* explain that "the daily constraints of insulin treatment often clash with the adolescent's fundamental drive for freedom and self sufficiency, [and] the physical and psychological changes the body goes through during the four to eight years of maturation during adolescence often make glucose control difficult."[36] Teens with other autoimmune diseases may also face difficulties because of conflicts with parents over who is responsible for daily care, and some lash out by refusing to follow their doctors' orders. This, of course, may worsen their physical condition.

Children and teens who must take medication while at school or who have to modify their activities are especially likely to feel resentful and may strongly resist following their doctors' recommendations. Many, to prevent teasing or having others feel sorry for them, do not want teachers and classmates to know about their illness. But in many cases, their parents need to inform school officials about what to do in an emergency, such as low blood sugar in diabetes or sudden flares in lupus, MS, and other diseases. While most friends and classmates are sympathetic and eager to help out, sometimes

The daily constraints of insulin treatment often clash with an adolescent's desire for freedom and self-sufficiency.

The Benefits of Support Groups

Many patients benefit from participating in support groups. According to the Lupus Foundation of America,

> The importance of support groups can be summarized as "The Three I's" they provide: Interaction, Information, and Inspiration. Patients have the opportunity to share personal experiences, obtain useful information, and listen to the ideas and advice of those in similar situations. The meeting room is a place where emotional catharsis is encouraged; where no one is judged, accused, or disbelieved because their disease is "unseen," where true empathy is the norm rather than the exception. Through focused discussions, support group leaders strive to help patients and loved ones to accept their circumstances, develop necessary coping skills, enhance the physician-patient relationship, and discover ways to maintain self-esteem and a sense of purpose amidst the complications imposed by chronic illness.

Lupus Foundation of America. "The Importance of Support Groups for the SLE Patient." www.lupus.org/education/topics/supportgroups.html.

Support groups are important because patients have the opportunity to share personal experiences, obtain useful information, and listen to the ideas and advice of others with similar afflictions.

kids do get teased about their condition. Leah, a teen with diabetes, told the Juvenile Diabetes Research Foundation (JDRF) that some classmates would say things like "There's the nerd with the needle." But Leah learned that responding with a remark such as "Wow, that's so original. I'll have to write that in my book of diabetes insults. I've never heard that"[37] quickly shut the teasers up.

Sometimes kids must miss school because of illness, and that can affect them academically and socially, too. Katie, a college student with Crohn's disease, writes, "I have had to withdraw from my college classes halfway through the semester and take time out of work because of stress-induced reactions. I have learned to reduce the number of classes I take per semester and to try to plan things out in advance to reduce the stress in my life. Having Crohn's is stressful enough without adding life into the mix."[38]

Stresses for Family Members

Besides being challenging for patients, autoimmune diseases also affect the lives of family members. Parents and spouses who must care for a patient may have to take time off work or even stop working entirely. A NIAID study found, for example, that over half of mothers of young children with diabetes have to stop working to care for the child full-time. This can create financial difficulties, especially with the high costs of treating these diseases.

Sometimes older children and teens who have an ill family member are faced with helping with patient care as well. Morgan, whose father was disabled by MS, learned to help care for him and her younger siblings starting when she was eleven. She managed to keep up her grades and participate in extracurricular activities anyway, but wrote that her father's illness added many challenges to her life: "This disease, the poison which runs through my father's nervous system, has also penetrated my heart. It has forced me to grow up too fast, face too many hard decisions and terrifying thoughts, and in the long run this disease will take my father away from me. As

I stand on the edge of the horizon looking off into adulthood, I know that this will always be a part of who I am."[39]

Siblings of children with autoimmune diseases may also face emotional difficulties. Some feel left out if parents pay more attention to the sick child. Others want to help but are not sure of what to do. Experts say parents can help siblings and a child with an illness adjust by treating the ill child just like everyone else as much as possible. The Arthritis Foundation advises, "Expect your child with arthritis to behave as correctly as other children and have the same responsibilities. Avoid giving her special privileges. Your child will benefit by doing chores that she is physically able to do."[40]

Methods of Coping

Medical experts, patients, and families have found many ways of coping with the challenges presented by autoimmune disorders. The most important way to make life easier is to accept the reality of the situation and realize that while no one can change the fact that the illness exists, it is possible to control other factors that contribute to the quality of life. Patients who make an effort to find a caring and competent doctor, educate themselves about their disease, partner with the doctor to establish the best possible therapy, and follow their treatment plan tend to cope better than those who do not. Those who accept the limitations a disease may impose, while still trying to live as fully as possible, also have a better quality of life. Olympic swimmer Gary Hall Jr., for example, was initially discouraged after doctors told him he could no longer swim competitively when he was diagnosed with diabetes in 1999. But then he found a doctor who taught him how to carefully monitor his condition during workouts and competitions. He frequently tested his blood sugar and always had snacks on hand, and he not only continued swimming but went on to win ten Olympic medals. Professional hockey player B.J. Crombeen, who also has diabetes, revealed in a Juvenile Diabetes Research Foundation publication that he refused to let the disease stop him from achieving his dream of playing pro hockey: "[My parents] just said, 'This is what you're going to have to do, and we're going to have to make it part of your life.' I said 'Okay' and went with it, rather than feeling sorry for myself."[41]

Another part of taking charge includes keeping overall health as good as possible by eating a well-balanced diet, getting sufficient sleep, and doing as much regular exercise as possible. Some patients with specific diseases must follow special diets—for instance, people with diabetes usually cannot eat sweets because they quickly raise blood sugar, those with celiac disease cannot eat anything containing gluten, and those with lupus must avoid eating alfalfa sprouts because they contain a chemical that worsens lupus. But people with most other autoimmune diseases are simply advised to follow a generally healthy diet that provides adequate protein, vitamins, and minerals.

The amount of exercise patients can do depends entirely on how severe their disease is. Some can barely walk, while others are able to jog, swim, or participate in other strenuous activities. Many patients also benefit from engaging in relaxation techniques like meditation, yoga, or tai chi to help ease pain as well as enhance mental peace.

Many patients report that participating in online or local support groups, which consist of others dealing with similar challenges, can be especially helpful for coping. Some support groups meet and exchange information about a disease and offer compassion and support when needed. Others may sponsor educational lectures or engage in advocacy efforts to promote public awareness and raise research funds for particular diseases.

Celebrity Advocates

Many celebrities affected by autoimmune disorders have used their fame to give advocacy groups a boost in their quest to bring attention to the suffering of patients and the need for increased research. Professional basketball players Charlie Villanueva and Austin Daye, for example, appeared in public service announcements about the need for increased awareness of the similarities among diverse autoimmune diseases.

Villanueva suffers from alopecia areata universalis, which causes the loss of all body hair, and Daye's mother has MS.

Pop star Nick Jonas has become a spokesperson for the JDRF and frequently offers encouragement to other teens and kids with the disease. He was also national chair of the 2010 JDRF Walk to Cure Diabetes and testified before the U.S. Congress about the need for research funding. Jonas finds that

Actress Kellie Martin holds a handbag she donated to The Old Bags Lupus Luncheon in Beverly Hills, California. Martin, who lost her sister to lupus, serves as a spokesperson for AARDA.

helping others helps him cope with his own diabetes. "I have this passion to be able to share with young people my age and be a positive light in a situation that might not be so positive,"[42] he says.

Former FBI agent Sue Thomas, who has MS and is also deaf, has used her celebrity status to fight for MS research. Thomas, who was the inspiration behind the popular TV show *Sue Thomas F.B.Eye*, says, "I've gone from being the FBI's secret weapon to being the weapon to destroy MS."[43] She is also involved in building a facility that trains service dogs to help people who have multiple disabilities. The service dog she has is trained to assist her both with her deafness (by serving as her ears) and with chores she cannot perform because of her MS.

Actress Kellie Martin, whose nineteen-year-old sister Heather died from lupus because doctors failed to diagnose the disease soon enough to help her, serves as an AARDA spokesperson. She frequently addresses medical, government, and patient groups about the need for accurate diagnosis, treatment, and research in the hope that others will not have to endure the heartache she and her family experienced. Indeed, advocates like Martin, along with patients and medical experts who see the impact of autoimmune diseases every day, have played a big role in shaping current and future education and research priorities.

CHAPTER FIVE

The Future

The millions of people who live with autoimmune disorders are well aware of the need for improved education, diagnosis, prevention, and treatment. Autoimmune diseases are expensive, painful, and unrelenting. The NIH estimates that health care costs for these diseases total about $150 billion per year in the United States alone, and experts expect this amount to increase dramatically as the number of people affected continues to rise. The associated emotional and physical suffering are incalculable. Since effective treatments exist for only about 10 percent of the known autoimmune diseases, doctors can currently do little to help many patients.

But despite their prevalence and impact, autoimmune diseases have historically been misunderstood and largely ignored by the public and by many medical experts. A 2010 AARDA report found that "today, fewer than 13% of Americans can name, unaided, an autoimmune disease,"[44] and research funding lags far behind that for other serious illnesses. The NIH budget for cancer research, for example, is ten times higher than that for autoimmune diseases, despite the fact that autoimmune diseases affect more individuals.

One NIH official called autoimmune disorders the "least investigated, most difficult to diagnose, and physically and emotionally painful diseases that face Americans today."[45] Thus, advocates are lobbying for more education and research funding, and scientists are engaged in ongoing research on causes, diagnosis, prevention, and treatment in an attempt to address the ever growing magnitude of these diseases in the future.

Progress in Awareness and Education

Some progress on these fronts has already been achieved. In March 2010 the U.S. Senate approved legislation designating March as "National Autoimmune Diseases Awareness Month" and increased the amount of federal research funding. Also in March 2010, NIH researchers and representatives from patient groups and pharmaceutical companies held the first Autoimmune Diseases Summit in Washington, D.C., to share information about patient needs, improvements in physician training, and current research.

Many citizen and advocacy groups have forced industries and the government to clean up some of the toxic waste sites suspected of causing autoimmune disease clusters.

The American Autoimmune Related Diseases Association (AARDA)

As the only national nonprofit organization devoted exclusively to the vast variety of autoimmune diseases, AARDA has made great strides in promoting awareness and research since its inception. "When AARDA was founded in 1992, there were roughly 67 known autoimmune diseases and another 20 strongly suspected of being autoimmune in nature. Yet, the term 'autoimmune' was unheard of and a virtual void existed in terms of any type of national focus or understanding that these diseases constituted a significant disease category," explained AARDA executive director Virginia T. Ladd in a 2010 press release. Since 1992 AARDA has begun many programs to help patients and to teach the public and medical professionals about the similarities among diverse autoimmune disorders. Some of their programs include:

- physician education conferences;

- a national awareness campaign;

- research funding;

- a toll-free national patient referral line;

- a quarterly newsletter;

- providing speakers for a variety of patient and scientific meetings;

- lobbying government for increased education and research funding.

Quoted in American Autoimmune Related Diseases Association. "Comprehensive Report on the Global State of Autoimmune Diseases Released for National Autoimmune Disease Awareness Month." www.aarda.org/press_release_display.php?ID=53.

Progress is also being made in addressing public concerns about environmental toxins that may be contributing to the rise in autoimmune diseases. Citizen and advocacy groups have forced industries and the government to clean up some of the toxic waste sites suspected of causing autoimmune disease clusters, and the EPA has initiated extensive research into determining which chemicals and consumer products are dangerous enough to ban. Several flame retardants, cleaning products, and pesticides have already been banned in some states and on a national level. Health warnings are now required on some chemicals.

Many studies are also under way to assess the effectiveness of certain educational programs in convincing patients to follow their doctors' orders. Researchers at University Hospital Case Medical Center in Ohio, for instance, are studying whether diabetes education classes and counseling sessions motivate teens with diabetes to wear new devices called continuous glucose monitors and to take other steps to achieve better control of their disease. Many preteens and teens have difficulty transitioning from relying on parents to administer treatment to taking charge themselves, and the researchers hope that improved education and support will help them adapt.

Research into Causes

Hand in hand with attempts to improve awareness and education, scientists are also conducting a great deal of research into causes, diagnosis, prevention, and treatment. Many studies are investigating how and why autoimmune diseases develop. Some scientists are studying the biochemical processes that cause specific diseases, while others are starting to focus on the basic biology and common triggers that underlie all autoimmune disorders. Noel R. Rose states in an AARDA article that he believes this newer focus is a positive step toward unraveling the mysteries of the autoimmune process:

> All of these diseases, diverse as they are, are related because they have the same etiology [cause]; they are all caused by autoimmunity. In my opinion, the only way we're

going to develop really effective treatments will be to treat the cause of the disease, not the symptoms. The symptoms are late; the symptoms are at the end of the train of events. We want to get on the train at the very beginning.[46]

In one study on causes, scientists at National Taiwan University are investigating whether defects in the way phagocytes clear dead cells from the body may play a role in autoimmunity. Studies on mice previously revealed that animals with genetic defects that lead to an inability to process and remove dead immune cells have an increased risk of developing diseases like lupus and arthritis. The researchers are hoping to identify which molecules on dead cells signal phagocytes to take action, and they are also studying how different genes affect the immune system's ability to judge which cells are dead and which are alive.

Research published in 2009 by doctors at the Weizmann Institute of Science in Israel sheds light on another possible biological mechanism in autoimmunity. The researchers found that white blood cells involved in an immune response to an infection or injury actually crawl along the lining of blood vessels, gripping this lining with tiny "legs" until they receive chemical signals telling them it is time to migrate to the site of the damage. They then exit the blood vessels and proceed to their destination. The investigators believe it may be possible to control an autoimmune attack by interrupting the ability of the "legs" to hold onto the blood vessel linings, and they are planning future studies to determine whether or not this is true.

Scientists at NIAID believe another factor that may play a role in autoimmunity is that mutations in a gene called the Fas gene appear to trigger the development of abnormal T cells known as double negative T cells. Double negative T cells lack two surface proteins that are needed for the cells to die and disintegrate after they have performed their duties. The researchers have shown that the accumulation of these abnormal T cells in the lymph nodes and spleen leads to autoimmune lymphoproliferative syndrome. They are investigating whether double negative T cells may be involved in causing other autoimmune diseases as well.

Many other studies are trying to establish how genes and environmental triggers interact to cause autoimmune disorders. Researchers at North Shore Long Island Jewish Health System in New York are performing blood tests on sisters of people with lupus to try to pinpoint these interactions. The investigators explain:

> Close relatives of people with these diseases are at greater risk of developing the same or another autoimmune disease. The study is designed to determine several things: If sisters of people with SLE make the same antibodies that are present in people with SLE, whether or not environmental factors affect the chances of developing these antibodies and if so what these environmental factors may be, [and] if the presence of these antibodies in healthy people leads to increased risk for the development of SLE.[47]

Research into Prevention and Diagnosis

Tests for autoantibodies in the blood of people who do not yet have an autoimmune disease may someday allow doctors not only to predict who is likely to develop one but also to intervene to prevent this from happening. Researchers at a variety of institutions affiliated with the worldwide Immune Tolerance Network are investigating many possible methods of prevention. Scientists at the National Institute of Diabetes and Digestive and Kidney Diseases are studying whether the monoclonal antibody teplizumab prevents diabetes in patients' relatives who show autoantibodies but have not yet developed symptoms. Previous studies indicate that teplizumab reduces decreases in insulin production if given to people with diabetes within a year after diagnosis, and the investigators believe it may help stop or slow the autoimmune destruction of islet cells in at-risk people as well.

Scientists at Sanofi Aventis Pharmaceuticals are evaluating whether an anti-inflammatory drug called teriflunomide can prevent full-blown MS from developing in patients who have experienced only one demyelinating episode. They are using magnetic resonance imaging (MRI) to assess whether plaques stop forming in the central nervous system, and they are also using standardized criteria to measure whether patients' disabilities stop or progress.

Improved methods of diagnosing autoimmune disorders early on in the disease process may also help doctors prevent disease progression before irreversible damage occurs. Scientists are developing new techniques for reliably identifying autoantibodies and other biochemical "markers" that indicate the presence of certain diseases. Researchers at the NIH Institute of Dental and Craniofacial Research, for example, are testing a new technique called luciferase immunoprecipitation (LIPS) to see how reliably it identifies a variety of autoantibodies. Scientists begin the LIPS laboratory test by fusing an enzyme called luciferase with a particular antigen. When an antibody in a patient's blood attaches to the antigen, the luciferase lights

Scientists at Sanofi Aventis Pharmaceuticals are evaluating the drug teriflunomide to see if it can prevent full-blown MS from developing.

up and reveals the presence and amount of the antibody. Tests have already shown that LIPS correctly identifies the SS-B autoantibodies associated with Sjogren's syndrome about 75 percent of the time. Previous tests identified this autoantibody only 50 percent of the time. The researchers are hoping LIPS will prove to be reliable for diagnosing other diseases as well.

Research into Treatment

Equally important as research into causes and diagnosis are attempts to improve treatment. One frustrating aspect of treatment for some diseases is that doctors cannot predict who will respond well or relapse after therapy stops, so they are often unsure of how long drug treatments should last. According to Ken Smith of the Cambridge Institute for Medical Research in England,

> When someone comes in with an autoimmune disease, we treat them all similarly because we have no way of telling in advance who will do badly and who will do well. Often when people end up suffering the toxic side effects of the treatment we don't know if they really needed it in the first place—but of course we could not risk treating them less intensively in case we failed to control their disease.[48]

In 2010, researchers at the University of Cambridge made some headway into possible methods of personalizing treatment. They discovered that different patterns of genes that control certain T cells called CD8+ T cells correspond to how likely patients with autoplasmic antibody-associated vasculitis are to relapse after initial successful treatment is stopped. This disease involves an autoimmune attack on neutrophils and leads to inflamed blood vessels and often to deadly kidney disease or stroke. About 30 percent of patients with this disease who are treated with immunosuppressive drugs die from drug-induced infections, so knowing who is not likely to relapse if the drugs are discontinued could potentially save many lives.

Related research is studying whether measuring blood levels of TNF and other proteins called calcium binding proteins

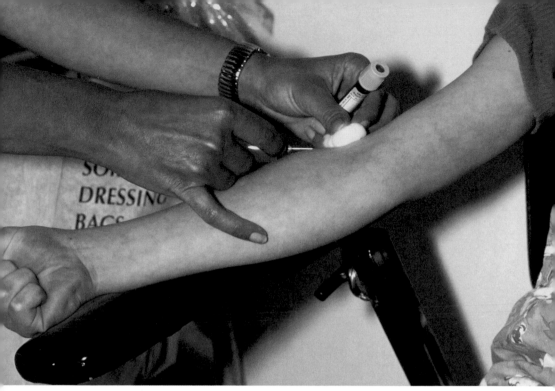

A doctor takes a blood sample from a patient to study blood levels of TNF and other proteins to help predict which children with juvenile arthritis are likely to remain in remission if treatment with anti-TNF drugs is discontinued.

(TNF and calcium binding proteins are involved in inflammation), along with screening for gene mutations associated with susceptibility to rheumatoid arthritis, can help predict which children with juvenile arthritis are likely to remain in remission if treatment with anti-TNF drugs is discontinued. No results have yet been published.

Research into New Drug Treatments

Other treatment research is focused on developing and testing new drugs for various autoimmune diseases. A major goal in this type of research is finding medications that suppress only certain parts of the immune system while not impacting its ability to fight infections and cancers.

Scientists at NIAMS have discovered that genetically engineering mice so they lack a protein called DR3 leads to improved symptoms in animals that have a disease similar to MS without suppressing the entire immune system. DR3 causes inflammation and is found on T cell receptors. The DR3-deficient mice showed reduced inflammation in their nervous systems but were still able to launch an effective immune response against numerous antigens. This suggests a possible target for new drugs that could safely reduce inflammation in people.

Researchers led by Denise Faustman at Massachusetts General Hospital in Boston have progressed to the point of testing a targeted drug called bacillus calmette-guerin (BCG) on humans with diabetes. BCG elevates the level of TNF-alpha and selectively kills only T cells that attack the self, while leaving other immune cells intact. Elevating the level of TNF-alpha to diminish autoimmunity seems counterintuitive to many medical experts, who note that many of the newer drugs used to treat autoimmune diseases are TNF inhibitors. For this reason, many doctors have ridiculed and questioned Faustman's approach. But Faustman and her colleagues stand by their findings, and

An electron micrograph shows the rod-shaped bacillus calmette-guerin (BCG) bacteria. BCG elevates the level of TNF-alpha and kills off only T cells that are attacking the body.

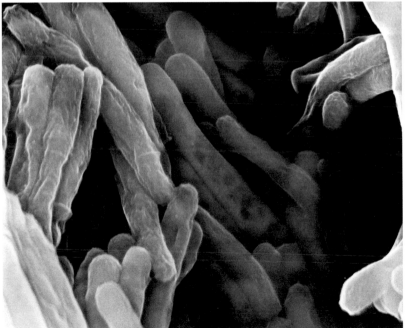

since 2001 have seen excellent results using TNF and TNF-boosting products in mice. In 2001, for example, they reported that administering TNF-alpha to mice with diabetes not only destroyed the T cells that were attacking the animals' islet cells but also allowed the islet cells to regenerate and produce insulin. Whether these results will occur in humans with diabetes remains to be seen.

Faustman states on her laboratory's website that if this new treatment is successful for diabetes, it could potentially be used for other autoimmune diseases as well: "We believe this could be a safer approach to treating autoimmunity, one that avoids or reduces the toxicity observed with existing therapies."[49]

Other Drugs Under Investigation

Other researchers are testing other new targeted therapies, primarily new monoclonal antibodies, and some are testing drugs already approved for other purposes to see if they are effective against certain autoimmune diseases.

One new monoclonal antibody is LY2127399. This drug inhibits the activity of a chemical called B cell activating factor. Tests on laboratory animals showed that LY2127399 reduced levels of this chemical and of autoantibodies without affecting other immune cells, and researchers at Eli Lilly and Company Pharmaceuticals are evaluating whether it safely reduces symptoms and disease progression in people with lupus.

Novartis Pharmaceuticals is testing two new drugs with novel modes of action on patients with MS to see whether the medications safely reduce brain plaques and disease progression. AIN457 is a monoclonal antibody that blocks the inflammatory cytokine interleukin-17. Novartis previously found it to be effective in treating rheumatoid arthritis. BAF312 is a new oral drug that prevents lymphocytes from migrating to inflamed sites in the body. Testing has not progressed far enough for the investigators to know whether it will be safe and effective.

Sometimes drugs already approved for other diseases can help people with certain autoimmune disorders, so researchers test these products as well as new drugs. Scientists at the National

Bringing New Drugs to Market

Researchers begin by developing new drugs in laboratories and testing their safety and effectiveness on laboratory animals. Once a drug passes these tests, doctors begin clinical trials, in which the drugs are tested on human volunteers. The U.S. Food and Drug Administration (FDA) and similar agencies in other countries regulate all aspects of drug testing and approval.

A drug must successfully undergo three phases of clinical trials before the FDA will approve it for sale. In phase one, a small group of patients, usually no more than ten or twenty, receive the new drug to help researchers determine what will be a safe, effective dose. In phase two, a larger group of about one hundred volunteers are given the drug over several years to further assess the drug's safety and effectiveness over an extended period of time. Phase three involves thousands of patients from a variety of locations, who are randomly assigned to one of two groups—an experimental group or a control group. Those in the experimental group receive the new drug, while those in the control group receive a placebo, or fake. All patients believe that they are receiving the new drug, and this way doctors can assess whether any positive results are due to the expectation of success rather than to the drug itself.

If a drug's benefits outweigh its risks and it is approved for sale, drug manufacturers will sometimes arrange phase four, or postmarket, studies to learn about long-term effects or to test whether the drug will be effective in combating other diseases.

Eye Institute, for example, are evaluating whether the immunosuppressive drug rituximab, currently used to treat cancer and rheumatoid arthritis, may be effective for treating autoimmune retinopathy, which involves an attack on cells in the retina of the eye. Currently, no effective treatments for this disease exist.

Doctors use artificial sex hormones to treat a variety of diseases. Since many autoimmune disorders affect far more women than men, many experts have hypothesized that such hormones may also be effective for treating certain autoimmune diseases, even though they can have side effects like raising the risk of breast cancer. Researchers at Sant'Andrea Hospital in Italy are currently testing whether adding the female hormones estrogen and progesterone to an interferon beta regimen helps reduce brain plaques and fatigue and improves mental functioning and quality of life in women with MS. Other researchers are testing these hormones on people with other autoimmune diseases.

Natural Remedies

Since so many existing treatment drugs have dangerous side effects, many patients seek safer natural compounds. Vitamin and mineral supplements are not regulated by the U.S. Food and Drug Administration, so they are often marketed without scientific proof of their safety and effectiveness. Thus, researchers are testing some of these products to see if they really work. Researchers at the State University of New York are testing an antioxidant (substance that prevents cell damage from molecules called free radicals) known as N-acetylcysteine to see whether it helps people with lupus. N-acetylcysteine, which is sold in health food stores, is a precursor of the naturally occurring antioxidant glutathione. Studies have shown that people with lupus have abnormally low levels of glutathione in their T cells, and some experts believe this deficiency may contribute to autoimmunity. The investigators are administering various doses of N-acetylcysteine to patients to see whether their symptoms improve and whether side effects from immunosuppressive drugs are also diminished.

Scientists at the U.S. Department of Veterans Affairs are testing whether another antioxidant called lipoic acid slows the progression of disability in people with certain types of MS. Lipoic acid is found in red meat, spinach, broccoli, potatoes, yams, carrots, beets, and yeast. The body also produces small amounts. Previous studies have shown that lipoic acid supplements help treat nerve damage in people with diabetes, and the researchers hope it will be effective in slowing the nerve damage that affects MS patients.

New Nondrug Treatments

Researchers are also exploring new nondrug treatments. Doctors at Albany Medical College in New York are testing whether a procedure called angioplasty is effective in removing plaques that block the jugular and azygos veins in some people with MS. This MS complication, known as chronic cerebrospinal venous insufficiency, prevents blood from draining from the central nervous system and exacerbates weakness,

In deep brain stimulation a physician inserts thin wires into a specific brain area and runs an electrical current through the wires. This treatment for Parkinson's disease is being used to see whether it helps MS patients who have severe tremors.

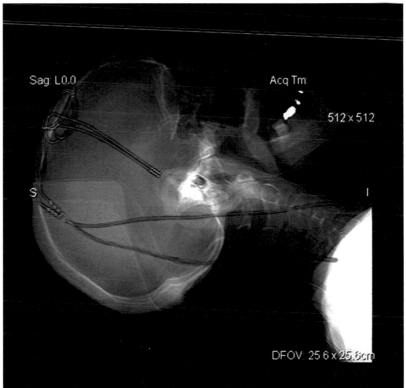

cognitive problems, and the inability to walk. Doctors have used angioplasty for many years to clear fatty deposits from arteries in people with heart disease. The procedure involves the physician threading a balloon into a blood vessel and inflating the balloon.

Other researchers are testing another existing technology called deep brain stimulation to see whether it helps people with MS who have severe tremors. Here, a physician inserts thin, coiled wires into specific brain areas and runs an electrical current through the wires. The procedure is currently used to treat tremors in people with Parkinson's disease who are not helped by drug treatments. It has many risks, however, including the possibility of worsening symptoms and further damaging the brain, so it is only used in critical cases.

Toward a Cure

Doctors and patients, of course, would prefer to be able to cure, rather than just treat, autoimmune diseases in the future, and several avenues of research are pursuing likely candidates for cures. Researchers in Israel are currently testing a newly developed computerized artificial pancreas called MD-Logic Artificial Pancreas to see whether it can effectively deliver insulin to people with diabetes when an electronic glucose sensor reveals that blood sugar levels are rising. Although this device would not restore beta cell function, it has the potential to free patients from daily insulin injections and glucose monitoring. The researchers state, "Theoretically, subcutaneous [under the skin] insulin pumps and glucose sensors attached to an artificial pancreas can mimic the activity of functioning pancreatic beta cells, with strict control of blood glucose levels."[50]

Other cure options being evaluated for diabetes include using genetic engineering techniques to manipulate genes that regulate beta cell growth, and identifying proteins that can promote such growth. Gene manipulation techniques are still being perfected and are not yet being employed in humans with autoimmune disorders, but investigators at Exsulin Corporation have developed a protein called Islet New Genesis Associated Protein (INGAP) Peptide that appears to stimulate

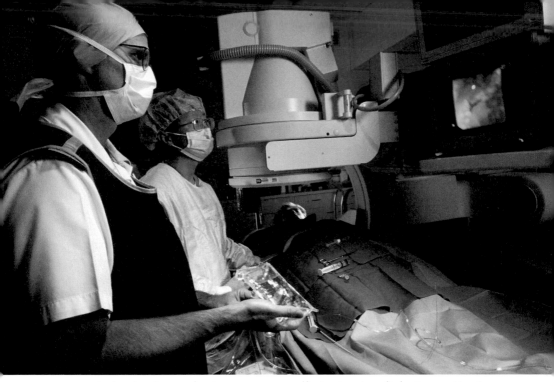

A doctor transplants pancreas cells to treat a diabetes patient. The procedure, if successful, will allow diabetics to stop injecting insulin.

beta cell growth. Clinical trials with INGAP Peptide are currently under way, and thus far it appears to be very safe.

Cell transplants are another area of intense investigation. Many researchers are testing whether transplanting donor beta cells into people with diabetes allows them to stop injecting insulin. Some patients thus far have not had to take artificial insulin for months or even years after the transplant, but the procedure fails in many other cases. Patients who receive a transplant must also take powerful immunosuppressive drugs to prevent their bodies from rejecting the transplanted cells.

Transplanting stem cells taken from the patients themselves gets around the rejection problem because the body will not reject these cells. Stem cells can be obtained from embryos, umbilical cord blood, or donor or patient blood or bone marrow and are then grown in a tissue culture. Due to controversy about the morality of using stem cells taken from embryos, for a while the government did not fund such research. But currently this research is being allowed to proceed because of its immense potential for curing many diseases.

Many scientists are investigating whether infusing stem cells intravenously into a patient results in the stem cells migrating to and repairing various diseased body parts. In some cases, doctors kill off a patient's existing immune cells with chemotherapy and radiation so the transplanted stem cells can "reboot" the immune system and hopefully stop an autoimmune attack entirely. This is a dangerous procedure, but it has worked in some instances. In addition to experimenting with stem cell transplants, doctors are also developing biochemical methods of coaxing stem cells to develop into specific types of body cells so they will be more likely to have therapeutic value for certain diseases.

Goals for the Future

Each research advance brings medical science closer to achieving the goals of understanding, preventing, and curing autoimmune diseases. Considering that sixty years ago doctors did not believe autoimmunity was even possible, many experts have pointed out that researchers have made remarkable progress in a relatively short period of time. However, NIAID sums up the consensus that much more work is needed in the future before these goals can be realized: "Despite our progress, we recognize that more needs to be done so that we may close the gaps in our knowledge and achieve our overall goal of reducing the rising toll of autoimmune disease."[51]

Notes

Introduction: A Rapidly Multiplying Problem

1. Quoted in Donna Jackson Nakazawa. *The Autoimmune Epidemic*. New York: Simon & Schuster, 2008, p. xvi.
2. Noel R. Rose. Interview by author, January 31, 2011.
3. Ahmet Hoke. Interview by author, January 13, 2011.

Chapter One: What Are Autoimmune Disorders?

4. Quoted in Nakazawa. *The Autoimmune Epidemic*, p. xvi.
5. National Institute of Arthritis and Musculoskeletal and Skin Diseases. "Autoimmune Diseases." www.niams.nih. gov/Health_info/Autoimmune/default.asp.
6. Dana K. Cassell and Noel R. Rose. *The Encyclopedia of Autoimmune Diseases*. New York: Facts On File, 2003, p. 64.
7. Robert G. Lahita. *Women and Autoimmune Disease*. New York: HarperCollins, 2004, p. 5.
8. National Institute of Allergy and Infectious Diseases. "Immune System." www.niaid.nih.gov/topics/immuneSystem/ pages/whatisimmunesystem.aspx.
9. Rose, interview.
10. National Institutes of Health. "Autoimmune Disorders." www.nih.gov/medlineplus/ency/article/000816.htm.
11. Quoted in Linda von Wartburg. "Type 1 Pop Star, Nick Jonas Tells His Story." *Diabetes Health*. www.diabetes health.com/read/2007/04/26/5150/type-1-pop-star-nick-jonas-tells-his-story.

Chapter Two: What Causes Autoimmune Disorders?

12. American Autoimmune Related Diseases Association. "Questions and Answers." www.aarda.org/q_and_a.php.

13. Quoted in Jeffrey Norris. "Good Cells Going Bad May Lead to Diabetes." *Science Café*, July 27, 2009. www.ucsf.edu/science-cafe/articles/autoimmune-diabetes-and-immune-system-regulatory-t-cells.

14. Quoted in American Autoimmune Related Diseases Association. "Sleep Disorder Identified as Autoimmune Disease." www.aarda.org/research_display.php?ID=71.

15. Quoted in American Autoimmune Related Diseases Association. "Sun and Autoimmune Disease in Women—a Connection." www.aarda.org/infocus_article.php?ID=60.

16. Lahita. *Women and Autoimmune Disease*, p. 29.

17. Quoted in Theresa Foy DiGeronimo. *New Hope for People with Lupus*. Roseville, CA: Prima, 2002, pp. 30–31.

18. Centers for Disease Control and Prevention. "Polybrominated Diphenyl Ethers (PBDEs)." www.atsdr.cdc.gov/toxfaqs/TF.asp?id=900&tid=183.

19. Renee M. Gardner et al. "Mercury Exposure, Serum Antinuclear/Antinucleolar Antibodies, and Serum Cytokine Levels in Mining Populations in Amazonian Brazil: A Cross-Sectional Study." *Environmental Research*, vol. 110, no. 4, February 21, 2010, pp. 345–354.

Chapter Three: Diagnosis and Treatment

20. Sjogren's Syndrome Foundation. "About Sjogren's Syndrome." www.sjogrens.org/home/about-sjogrens-syndrome.

21. American Autoimmune Related Diseases Association. "Autoimmunity: A Major Women's Health Issue." www.aarda.org/women_and_autoimmunity.php.

22. Lisa. "Some Days I Couldn't Get Out of Bed Due to Pain." Health.com. www.health.com/health/condition-article/0,,20385796,00.html.

23. American Autoimmune Related Diseases Association. "Questions and Answers."

24. Quoted in American Autoimmune Related Diseases Association. "What Are TNF-Alpha Inhibitors? What Should Patients Know?" www.aarda.org/infocus_article.php?ID=61.

25. Lahita. *Women and Autoimmune Disease*, pp. 245–246.

26. Quoted in National Multiple Sclerosis Society. "Clear Thinking About Complementary and Alternative Medi-

cine." www.nationalmssociety.org/about-multiple-
sclerosis/what-we-know-about-ms/treatments/comple
mentary--alternative-medicine/index.aspx.

Chapter Four: Living with Autoimmune Disorders

27. National Institute of Allergy and Infectious Diseases.
"Progress in Autoimmune Diseases Research." www.ni
aid.nih.gov/topics/autoimmune/Documents/adccfinal.pdf.
28. American Autoimmune Related Diseases Association.
"Coping with Autoimmunity." www.aarda.org/coping.php.
29. Quoted in Von Wartburg. "Type 1 Pop Star, Nick Jonas
Tells His Story."
30. Lisa. "Some Days I Couldn't Get Out of Bed Due to Pain."
31. Quoted in Nakazawa. *The Autoimmune Epidemic*, p. 32.
32. Quoted in St. Thomas's Lupus Trust. "Helen's Story."
www.lupus.org.uk/patients/helen.html.
33. Lisa. "Some Days I Couldn't Get Out of Bed Due to Pain."
34. Arthritis Foundation. "Dealing with Emotional Issues." www.arthritis.org/disease-center.php?disease_
id=38&df=resources.
35. Quoted in GirlsHealth.gov. "Illness and Disability." www
.girlshealth.gov/disability/types/index.cfm.
36. Cassell and Rose. *The Encyclopedia of Autoimmune Diseases*, p. 5.
37. Quoted in Juvenile Diabetes Research Foundation. "Diabetes in School." http://kids.jdrf.org/index.
cfm?fuseaction=home.viewPage&page_id=F05ADF39-
2A5E-7B6E-146315DDA27A7EDB.
38. Quoted in Care New England Health System. "Some
Nights It's Easier to Sleep in the Tub." www.carenew
england.org/body.cfm?id=84&action=detail&ref=56.
39. Quoted in National Multiple Sclerosis Society. "My Dad Is
My Hero." www.nationalmssociety.org/online-community/
personal-stories/morgan-ray/index.aspx.
40. Arthritis Foundation. "Dealing with Emotional Issues."
41. Quoted in Julie Mettenberg with Jodi Newcorn. "Not
Singin' the Blues: Hockey Right-Winger B.J. Crombeen
Plays for St. Louis, Despite Living with Diabetes Since

Age Nine." JDRF Kids Online. http://kids.jdrf.org/index.
cfm?fuseaction=home.viewPage&page_id=16AFD2B1-
1321-C844-13A2E55F69E8D4E4.

42. Quoted in Von Wartburg. "Type 1 Pop Star, Nick Jonas
Tells His Story."

43. Quoted in National Multiple Sclerosis Society. "Sue
Thomas Can't Quit Finding New Ways to Inspire." www
.nationalmssociety.org/online-community/personal-stories/
sue-thomas/index.aspx.

Chapter Five: The Future

44. Quoted in American Autoimmune Related Diseases Association. "Senate Resolution 372 Designates March 'National Autoimmune Diseases Awareness Month.'" www.
aarda.org/press_release_display.php?ID=54.

45. Quoted in Cassell and Rose. *The Encyclopedia of Autoimmune Diseases*, p. xvi.

46. Noel R. Rose. "The Common Thread." American Autoimmune Related Diseases Association. www.aarda.org/com
mon_thread_page2.php.

47. Clinical Trials.gov. "Autoimmunity in Sisters of Lupus Patients (SisSLE)." http://clinicaltrials.gov/ct2/show/NCT010
76101?recr=Open&cond=%22Autoimmune+Diseases%22&
rank=40.

48. Quoted in Mun-Keat Looi. "'Personalising' Autoimmune
Disease Treatments." Wellcome Trust, August 5, 2010.
http://wellcometrust.wordpress.com/2010/08/05/personal
ising-autoimmune-disease-treatments.

49. Denise Faustman. *Faustman Lab Newsletter*, Massachusetts General Hospital. www.faustmanlab.org/docs/news
letters/EmailBlast061410.pdf.

50. Clinical Trials Feeds. "Overnight MD-Logic." http://clinical
trialsfeeds.org/clinical-trials/show/NCT01238406.

51. National Institute of Allergy and Infectious Diseases.
"Progress in Autoimmune Disease Research."

Glossary

antibody: A chemical produced by the immune system to attack a specific antigen.

antigen: A foreign protein, substance, or organism that stimulates an attack by the immune system.

autoantibody: An antibody that is directed against one or more of a person's own proteins.

autoimmune: A body's cells and tissues being attacked by its own immune system.

biologic: A genetically engineered drug designed to target specific molecules.

chromosome: A wormlike body in the center of a cell where genes are found.

chronic: Long-term.

complement: Proteins active in the immune system.

cytokine: A chemical messenger in the immune system.

flare: Sudden worsening of symptoms.

gene: Part of a chromosome that transmits hereditary information.

immune system: The network of cells, tissues, and organs that defend the body from invasion.

immunosuppressive: A drug that inhibits the immune system.

leukocyte: White blood cell.

lymphatic system: A network of vessels and cells important in immune defense.

lymphocyte: A type of white blood cell important in the immune system.

phagocyte: Scavenger white blood cell.

relapse: Recurrence of disease or symptoms.

remission: Disappearance or marked improvement of disease symptoms.

stem cell: An immature cell that can mature into any type of body cell.

Organizations to Contact

American Autoimmune Related Diseases Association (AARDA)

22100 Gratiot Ave.
East Detroit, MI 48021
phone: (586) 776-3900
website: www.aarda.org

As the only national nonprofit organization dedicated to the wide spectrum of autoimmune diseases, AARDA offers information and support on all aspects of these disorders, including information on specific diseases.

National Institute of Allergy and Infectious Diseases (NIAID)

NIAID Office of Communications and Government Relations
6610 Rockledge Dr., MSC 6612
Bethesda, MD 20892-6612
phone: (301) 496-5717; toll-free: (866) 284-4107
website: www.niaid.nih.gov

NIAID is a government agency that supports and conducts research on many autoimmune diseases and provides information on all aspects of these diseases.

National Institute of Arthritis and Musculoskeletal and Skin Diseases (NIAMS)

Information Clearinghouse
National Institutes of Health
1 AMS Circle
Bethesda, MD 20892-3675
website: www.niams.nih.gov

NIAMS is a government agency that supports and conducts research into many autoimmune diseases and provides information on research and other disease topics.

The National Women's Health Information Center

U.S. Department of Health and Human Services
Office on Women's Health
phone: (800) 994-9662
website: http://womenshealth.gov

Since many autoimmune disorders affect mostly women, the National Women's Health Information Center offers extensive information on all aspects of autoimmune disorders.

For More Information

Books

Faith Hickman Brynie. *101 Questions About Your Immune System*. Minneapolis: Twenty-First Century, 2000. Answers teens' questions about the immune system in an easy-to-understand format.

Jacqueline Langworth. *Perspectives on Diseases and Disorders: Autoimmune Diseases*. Detroit: Greenhaven, 2011. Written for teens; provides opposing viewpoints and personal perspectives on autoimmune diseases.

Kelly Rouba. *Juvenile Arthritis: The Ultimate Teen Guide*. Lanham, MD: Scarecrow, 2009. A self-help guide for teens with arthritis.

Terry L. Smith. *Frequently Asked Questions About Celiac Disease*. New York: Rosen, 2006. Written for teens; overview of celiac disease.

Barbara Stahura. *Diseases and Disorders: Diabetes*. Detroit: Lucent, 2009. Written for teens about all aspects of diabetes.

Periodicals

Jeff Pearlman. "Like a Rock." *Sports Illustrated*, April 16, 2001. Interview with professional baseball player Tim Raines about his lupus.

Linda Von Wartburg. "Type 1 Pop Star, Nick Jonas Tells His Story," *Diabetes Health Magazine*, April 27, 2007. Interview with pop star Nick Jonas about his diabetes.

Websites

Care New England Health System, "Some Nights It's Easier to Sleep in the Tub" (www.carenewengland.org/body .cfm?id=84&action=detail&ref=56). Personal experience article written by a college student with Crohn's disease.

Children's Hospital Boston, "Autoimmune Diseases" (www .childrenshospital.org/az/Site614/mainpageS614P0.html). Hospital website discusses autoimmune diseases in an easy-to-understand fashion.

Girls Health, "Illness and Disability" (www.girlshealth.gov/ disability/index.cfm). Government website for teen girls about living with chronic illnesses in general; contains useful information applicable to living with autoimmune disorders.

Teens Health from Nemours, "Immune System" (http://kids health.org/teen/your_body/body_basics/immune.html). Teen website talks about how the immune system works and distinguishes different types of immune diseases.

Index

Picture Credits

Cover: Copyright © Steve Oh, M.S./Phototake—All rights reserved
Aaron Haupt/Photo Researchers, Inc., 9
Alex Bartel/Photo Researchers, Inc., 88
AP Images/Gerald Herbert, 66
AP Images/Robert F. Bukaty, 63
BSIP/Photo Researchers, Inc., 69
© Caro/Alamy, 86
Cecilia Magill/Photo Researchers, Inc., 71
David R. Frazier/Photo Researchers, Inc., 81
Dr. P. Marazzi/Photo Researchers, Inc., 57
Gale, Cengage, 7, 31
GARO/PHANIE/Photo Researchers, Inc., 54
G. Murti/Photo Researchers, Inc., 36
© Indigo Images/Alamy, 73
Janine Wiedel Photolibrary/Alamy, 62
Jon Kopaloff/FilmMagic/Getty Images, 78
Lea Paterson/Photo Researchers, Inc., 41
Mark Burnett/Photo Researchers, Inc., 45
Medical Body Scans/Photo Researchers, Inc., 93
© Medical-on-Line/Alamy, 39
Medi-Mation Ltd/Photo Researchers, Inc., 29
Michael Donne/Photo Researchers, Inc., 48
Omikron/Photo Researchers, Inc., 15
Popperfoto/Getty Images, 21
Richard T. Nowitz/Photo Researchers, Inc., 95
Scott Camazine/Photo Researchers, Inc., 26
Southern Illinois University/Photo Researchers, Inc., 34
SPL/Photo Researchers, Inc., 50, 89
3D4Medical/Photo Researchers, Inc., 12, 16, 24, 32
Will & Deni McIntyre/Photo Researchers, Inc., 74

About the Author

Melissa Abramovitz has been writing books, magazine articles, poems, and short stories for children, teens, and adults for twenty-five years. Many of her works are on health topics.

She grew up in San Diego, California, and developed an interest in medical issues as a teenager. At one time she thought she wanted to become a doctor but earned a degree in psychology from the University of California at San Diego in 1976 and began writing professionally in 1986 to allow her to be an at-home mom when her two children were small.